REBOOT

REBOOT

HOW TO PUT JOY BACK INTO TROUBLED TECHNOLOGY PROJECTS

GANAPATHY IYER

ISBN: 978-0-473-55239-8 (print)
ISBN: 978-0-473-55240-4 (ebook)

Cover Design by *Wordzworth.com*

Editing by Jessica Hoadley

For information about this title contact:
gi@gdconsulting.co.nz

Contents

The team that made this possible

Thank you –

To you – the project sponsor and project manager at the helm of a troubled project – for inspiring me to write this.

To my wife Dipali, son Balaark and our families. Also in loving memory of my father in law who was keen to read this book but passed away days before its publication.

To my colleagues and friends from the numerous institutions and organisations I have had the privilege to be associated with, for helping me find myself.

To Lynne Cazaly whose book writing programme I signed up to while writing this book. You are an awesome human. Your constant guidance, appreciation and encouragement went a long way in me getting this done.

To the Thought Leaders Business School and the tribe of generosity – your numerous and ever-increasing ways of inspiring me to be myself and use the power of my thoughts to serve others have been awesome.

To some of the best leaders I have had an opportunity to work with, I appreciate the wisdom you have passed on as I found my feet.

To my wonderful clients – for shaping my empathy and consideration for the team.

To Deepak Pratap – my friend, colleague and, in weird ways, mentor, for all the amazing conversations that have helped shape this book.

It is my sincere hope that this work will help project leaders and professionals across the world put joy and life back into troubled projects.

Why this and why now?

Projects spur growth for all their constituents.

Be it organisations that undertake these projects, individuals who lead them, team members who contribute to outcomes, suppliers who participate in them, projects provide that necessary shift to each one of them in multiple ways.

Whether it is opening up new channels for growth, improving the efficiency and effectiveness of how you serve your customers or how you engage and empower your employees, projects that are appropriately selected and effectively executed make a huge difference in improving our lives.

Yet, for all the potential they hold, project success rates have been languishing around the 1/3rd mark for decades with little to no improvement. The advent of numerous methodologies including agile have sparked excitement and the hope that success rates on projects can be significantly lifted. While evolving methods have contributed to some extent in improving success rates, they are nowhere close to justifying the massive amount of effort, time and cost poured into them.

Sure, they have provided a fillip to the economy by means of training organisations, certification shops and more, but meaningful results that can sustain have been slow to come through. Scrum masters, agile coaches and a number of such positions have come up and positioned themselves as the saviour for projects in trouble. Yet we haven't moved far ahead, and these positions have just added to the list of roles we have had on projects.

Another significant shift in projects has been the rising number of technology-based initiatives. With rapid evolution in technology and the internet, projects involving replacement of older technology and procurement of new ones have started to occupy a significant percentage of projects being undertaken by organisations across the world.

Try finding an organisation that doesn't have a digital transformation running in any part of the world and you will see what I mean.

Surveys done by numerous organisations / publications including McKinsey, Gallup, Harvard Business Review, Project Management Institute and others have found IT projects to be notorious when it comes to cost, schedule overruns and under delivery of promised value.

According to a McKinsey research[1] 17% of IT projects go so bad that they can threaten the very existence of organisations.

Throughout my career, I have seen the good and bad side of projects. I have read numerous surveys citing appalling statistics on project success rates and beaming almost the same reasons for failure repeatedly.

As I worked on more projects, it became evident to me that projects done well, can be liberating for people and organisations, allowing them to shift significantly in their areas of work. Done poorly, they can threaten existence and reputation.

The pain, anxiety, stress, fear and overall impact a troubled IT project can have on people is significant and none more than the project leadership (the sponsor(s) and the project manager). For a lot of them an IT project gone wrong can spell doom for their careers.

Troubled projects can be a double whammy when it comes to draining precious organisational assets as well as distracting organisations from their core operations. However they can also be a catalyst to spur us towards unprecedented growth.

The journey to recover a troubled project of any nature is painful and exhausting. However, done well, it can be an extremely fulfilling experience for all concerned.

The availability of a framework to go about understanding what ails an IT project and then recovering it would make this task less painful and more effective.

That is the purpose of this book.

Who is this book for?

This book is best suited for the project sponsor and project manager leading a technology enabled transformation project, especially one that involves deploying a packaged software application including Software as a Service (Saas).

If you are running an ERP, CRM, MDM or HCM(HRIS) implementation, this is for you.

This book aims to equip both these individuals with a framework that can be applied to help recover an ailing project (or elegantly put it to rest) with care.

Will this book be of use to others? I believe so.

Sponsors of other types of projects, project / programme managers and project team members working on any technology enabled transformation project will find this useful if they are amid a troubled project.

The challenge this book solves.

If I had to summarise this book in a single line, I would say this book helps you successfully navigate the first 4-6 weeks of being on or walking into a troubled technology enabled transformation project.

It is never a joy walking into a troubled project. The first 4-6 weeks into a troubled project are extremely stressful. From stakeholders up in arms to a disillusioned project team; from a schedule gone awry to a dwindling budget envelope; from the hurt of broken promises to extreme personal stress, the first few weeks of being in a troubled project are a test a project leader's character.

This is not for everyone and there is no negativity associated with saying this is not for me. However, if this is the situation you find yourself in and are keen to get stuck in and change things for the better, this book is for you.

This book is aimed at taking your project from trouble to joy.

The CARE framework

Based on my experience of dealing with troubled projects, I have outlined the 4 stage CARE (**C**onfess, **A**ct, **R**esolve, **E**xecute) framework to recover or elegantly close troubled projects.

The stages are as follows:

1 **Confess** – For a troubled project, this is the most critical phase. This is where we acknowledge we have a problem and unpack the magnitude and causes of the problem.

2 **Act** – In this stage, we take action (usually over 4–6 weeks) to adjust and align all the factors that will help us put joy and life back into this project.

3 **Resolve** – Decision time. Here we use the factors to help us decide whether to progress or not.

4 **Execute** – This phase ensures we do not repeat things that landed us in a troubled project in the first place.

Throughout these stages, I believe, there are 6 factors that need to be addressed to significantly enhance the probability of successful project recovery.

Six factors for success

Helping recover troubled projects over the years has helped me learn that the following 6 factors are key to recovering a troubled project:

1 A destination worth visiting.

2 A journey worth undertaking.

3 People who care.

4 Connections that click.

5 Money we need.

6 Rules of engagement

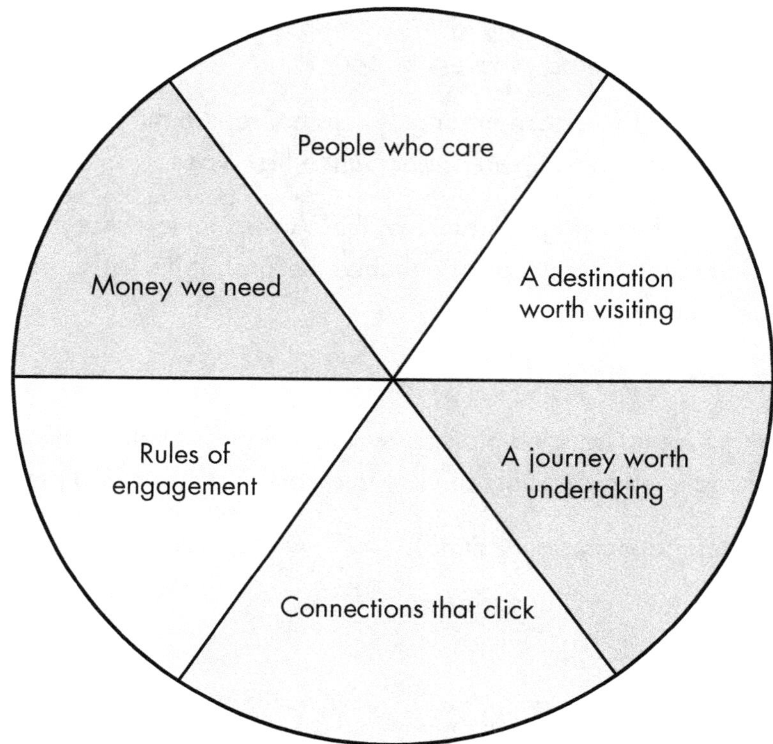

Figure 1.   Six factors for project success

I liken these to the making of a wood-fired pizza in a restaurant. Just like a successful project, making a pizza requires a combination of ingredients, the right environment, a knowledgeable chef and assistants, and customers willing to wait and pay for the result.

Remove any of these from the equation and the whole experience may fail.

This book will help you:

1   Be aware of aspects that cause projects to turn distressed.

2   Understand the 6 factors you have, to recover troubled projects.

3 Understand the CARE framework to use these 6 factors in helping you recover your project.

4 Navigate through a troubled project recovery, equipped with a guided framework.

5 Involve relevant people in appropriate capacity to deliver effective project outcomes.

On the other side of following the framework and the factors outlined in this book, you should be able to:

1 Reset a project successfully to deliver to stated outcomes.

2 Enable appropriate people to contribute their best work as well as enjoy themselves and grow.

3 Be more aware of the project and be able to sight signs of trouble early.

4 Manage project accountabilities, relationships and communications more effectively.

5 Set yourself up to land projects successfully.

This book does not presume an agile or waterfall delivery and can be applied equally to projects leveraging either methodologies.

It could also help you envisage some of the key things to consider while structuring projects in the first place so that they don't become troubled, but that is not the prime purpose of this book.

A note on language

While there are key differences between a project and a programme, I choose to refer to them as projects throughout this book. This is for convenience; the principles described in this book can well be applied to programmes as well.

How to use this book

There are possibly two reasons you picked this book:

1   You are leading a troubled project and looking for ways to recover –

    a   If you are in this situation, you are likely to derive most benefit from this book by going through the book by the phases – Confess, Act, Resolve, Execute.

    b   As you go through this, I would recommend you take actions suggested in each section.

    c   Within the phases, you can focus on the sections that worry you the most and come to the rest later.

2   You are an aspiring project manager who wants to build their reputation and mettle rescuing troubled projects OR You are leading a project that is not troubled but want to be more aware of the signs of trouble OR You are part of a project team and want to know more about projects.

    a   Start with the CONFESS phase as it will lay bare the anatomy of troubled projects. The examples, case studies and stories will help you build awareness of things to look out for, if and when (hopefully not soon ☺) you find yourself in that situation.

    b   I would also recommend you follow the sequence outlined within the CONFESS phase so that you are armed with a ready diagnostic to analyse a troubled project.

Introduction

Picture this……

You have championed a human capital management (HCM) or human resource information system (HRIS) solution implementation for your organisation that you truly believe will enhance the employee experience. Perhaps it will allow employees to access their leave information on their phone or view their payslips on the go. It might give managers insights about their team and how they could improve engagement.

You took great pains to get this project off the ground and invested yourself to champion it.

And now you are wondering what went wrong. You've got a project that has missed key dates, people at each other's throats and the company bleeding money on the project.

You worry about landing this project in a state where employee salaries are impacted and some of the things, they care about are severely disrupted!

You get a lot of artefacts and reports but cannot make out where the project is at and what ails it.

There seems to be no way out. You are bombarded with escalations. The suppliers you trusted as genuine partners seem disinterested and are handing you change requests seeking more funding, and your peers and leadership are beginning to ask questions.

Your outlook has been reduced to getting the project across the line instead of enabling the value you sought to unlock at the start.

You are extremely stressed about the project, its impact on people and the toll it is taking on you.

Not a pleasant situation, right?

This could be any other technology enabled project you have championed. It could be an ERP or CRM implementation for that matter.

I mentioned earlier in this book that projects have a notorious success rate of about one in three. The other thing to note here is a significant portion of such projects for organisations happen to be technology enabled.

Read that again: only one-third of projects are deemed successful.

Now those figures are definitely better than playing lotto, where the odds of hitting the jackpot are next to negligible. So, should we be content with this?

No. We do not spend hundreds, thousands or millions of dollars at a time in buying lotto tickets, and the next lotto draw is always just around the corner.

Projects, however, are a different ball game. Projects can be very expensive and time consuming and as a project sponsor or leader, you do not do the same type of projects often.

The failure of two-thirds of projects is not good enough. No one sets up a project visualising it to fail and no one walks away smiling at a project failure; instead, it creates blame, despair, stress and bad blood.

So, what can we do when find ourselves in the midst of a troubled project?

Let's start by exploring the symptoms of a troubled project:

Symptoms of a troubled project

When I first look at troubled projects, I typically see some of the following. Do these look familiar to you?

- **Meaningless outputs** (content not context). There may be a plethora of outputs (such as solution architecture, project charters, requirements documents and, lest the agile enthusiasts be disillusioned, user stories, product backlog items, Kanban boards) but you still can't get a clear picture of what is being achieved.

- **Different views.** Different people (or 'actors') give you different views of where they think you are on the project journey. It is a struggle to see who is in charge and what direction is the project pursuing.

- **Lack of clarity** (context). 'We are meeting to get clarity.' You hear the word 'clarity' being thrown around with magnanimity and yet it seems non-existent.

- **Excess waiting.** 'I am waiting on [Jo and Mo] to provide me with inputs so that I can progress.' While waiting on someone to help you move your work along is not uncommon on projects, the frequency seems to go up exponentially on troubled projects. Everybody seems to be waiting for somebody to provide something for them to move ahead.

- **Too much, or lack of, information.** A lot of potentially irrelevant information is being requested, which illustrates a lack of understanding of what is required. You might hear many different iterations of 'I need access to this folder.'

- **Jargon.** Jargon is unnecessary complicated language, used to sound impressive, rather than to help communication. It's out of control in some organisations. The best one I heard was a position called a 'de-escalation architect' and it had me almost falling off my chair. According to a good colleague, the de-escalation architect is employed to listen to your work problems and then remind you of world hunger to give you perspective. Jargon rarely helps a project succeed – the language needs to be plain and understandable. You will find a lot of it on a troubled project.

- ***Heightened emotions.*** On a troubled project, every request for clarity or context seems to stir some extremely passionate and emotional responses, especially if it is perceived as being accusatory or scrutinising.

- ***Meetings.*** Too many or too few but very disparate and inconsistent with a lot of key attendees missing and irrelevant ones present.

- **Emails.** Flying all around with a whole lot of content enough to drown the best of swimmers.

- **Personalities.** – Suddenly everyone knows how they could do someone else's job better, often trying to solution things beyond their remit.

The above list is by no means exhaustive but summarises some of the most common themes you are likely to encounter with increasing regularity on a troubled project.

Now that we have explored the symptoms of a troubled project, let's get straight into the recovery process.

Let's accord some CARE to your troubled project... read on......

1

CONFESS

1.1   A destination worth visiting?

Welcome to the CONFESS stage and the start of your recovery mission.

The first of the six factors to evaluate is whether the project can or will be 'a destination worth visiting'. This means you need to be able to discuss and articulate:

- **Product or service** – What will your project deliver?

- **Outcomes** – What will the product or service enable? Which organisational strategy does it align to?

- **People** – Who will benefit from it and do they care?

My wife and I once went to the local shopping mall with our son. Each of us had an idea of what we wanted to achieve out of our trip and the initial few minutes in the mall were pleasant. But then it all went south.

After three and a half hours, we had milk, eggs, fruits and a LEGO set. We also had a dejected woman, a grumpy guy and a kid who was happy as Larry.

Once we all calmed down a bit, we had some reflection time and landed on the following:

- My wife and I did not have a view of what we really wanted from the trip and what would tell us we have achieved it.

- We did not bother telling each other what our sense of fulfilment would look like and hence became tired, frustrated and grumpy.

- Our son was pretty clear – he wanted a LEGO set. Food was coincidental. He got both and was the happiest amongst us.

I am sure all of you have experienced some variation of this story and know how frustrating and unfulfilling it can be.

Without communication and clarity on the desired outcomes ('destination') this can easily happen within a project.

It's common for your key stakeholder groups to have different ideas about what they will get at the end of the project, and what it will enable for them. Understanding what these are is key. Don't take more than a day or two, but ensure you communicate with the important groups and write down their views and opinions – this is what you'll refer to later in the ACT phase.

You should also list the (relevant) artefacts that exist to support what people are saying about the project's destination.

Irrelevant artefacts are like the hand from the grave. Unless you bury them in concrete with no escape route, they will keep popping over and over to drain the energy out of your project and breed disillusionment.

National Grid USA[1], an electricity and gas distributor, embarked on an SAP implementation journey in 2007 and, years later, having endured Hurricane Sandy and its impact, ended up spending close to $585 million to clean up what was a troubled implementation.

While there are always a number of reasons why projects become troubled, one that stood out from Henrico Dolfing's analysis of this project in his eBook *Project Failure Case Studies* was the fact that there was limited validation of what the end outputs and outcomes would look like at the beginning and during the project. The case study points to factors like an overly ambitious design and limited availability of personnel due to ambitious business agendas in its dissection of the project.

Since then, National Grid has been through a massive legal battle with its suppliers and resolved differences. However, you can only imagine the stress and anxiety this would have caused when it all transpired.

One additional point to consider when it comes to understanding what your project will deliver and how it fits with the organisational strategy is risk. Without making this a big sermon on risk management, it is recommended to spend some time understanding risks that are relevant to your project and what they mean to the project as well as the organisation and individuals.

Much as risk is stated explicitly in this section, it applies throughout a project across every aspect and needs to be considered actively as you navigate through recovering your project.

A good set of questions to ask regarding risk at every stage of the project:

- What risks exist and are relevant?

- What will be the result of those risks eventualising?

- Does the project team have a conscious mitigation approach to them and are they sufficient to cover the impacts of the risk materialising?

Recap and actions

The essence of this chapter:

- Understand and uncover what your project will deliver.

Key questions to consider:

- What will your project deliver?

- What will the product or service enable? Which organisational strategy does it align to?

- Who will benefit from it and do they care?

- What risks are relevant and what do they mean.

To do:

1 Get input from all the appropriate and relevant groups of people about their expected outcomes.

2 Document their views and opinions (you may need to enable changing them later).

3 Jot down all the artefacts/documents that exist to support/ oppose their views.

To *not* do:

- Do not try to create outputs and outcomes on the fly.

- Do not assign blame (I am assuming the intention is to get the project back on track) on individuals or teams; an air crash is never caused by one reason. It is always a series of events that compound and cascade into an uncontrollable disaster.

- Do not be defensive about the state of things you find yourself in.

One must-read

- PMI conference paper – Bonghez, S. & Pop, R. (2016). Elephant on Thin Ice: Navigating Complexity through Project Culture. Paper presented at PMI® Global Congress 2016— EMEA, Barcelona, Spain. Newtown Square, PA: Project Management Institute.[2] (*https://www.pmi.org/learning/ library/navigating-complexity-project-culture-10181*)

1.2   A journey worth undertaking

My school days were joyful and carefree. I remember always rushing in just before the school bell rang and settling into my desk for morning prayers followed by attendance.

That good old bell was a feature of my school days – someone rang it at the start of the day, at the end of each class, recess and lunch, and then finally to signify the end of school.

Bear with me: I use this story whenever I find myself called in to support a troubled project.

The school day had a journey, or a 'story'.

- It had a clear start (think *ding ding ding ding*)
- It had a clear end (again *ding ding ding ding* – much more vigorously)
- It had visible stops throughout the day (generally a single *ding*)

The bell led us through the journey or 'story' of the school day and provided structure. We looked forward to the breaks and we loved the end.

This is key to a successful project. Uncovering a story or visualising a journey is the best way to become aware of whether a project is on track or not.

As part of the CONFESS stage within a troubled project, you will be well served to look for this journey. A good journey or story must include the start, the end and visible stops along the way.

But how do you know if you have a story and if the journey is a good one?

The best way is to start at the end.

Two simple questions should get you started:

- What is your go-live date?

- What is your project closeout date?

The response to these will give you great visibility on the existence of a planned journey within a project.

If you hear responses like 'We plan to go live sometime in May' or 'We are working through that,' you immediately know that there is an opportunity in this project to build a compelling journey (this is if you choose to continue with the project).

I often get thrown a curve ball about the project being delivered in an agile manner. I have two responses to this. If it is a typical software development project where you have squads/scrum teams delivering incremental functionality, then your release dates for those features into production form your go-live dates. If you are deploying a commercial off-the-shelf (COTS) packaged application (it doesn't matter if it is cloud-based or on premise) then you still need a clear go-live date. As far as the project closeout date is concerned, it is simple – when will the business as usual operations team be in complete charge of this solution?

Imagine you do get a concrete response on the go-live date, for example 18 June 2018. (I chose this date because we went live with a massive HCM payroll implementation on that day for a local government agency in NZ). The next question would be: when are the stops? (Think back to the school bell between classes, recess and lunch). This is not an irrelevant icebreaker question. The response to this question starts to unravel key challenges you are likely to encounter in setting this journey right.

It is also worth asking what these stops will signify. What will you have achieved on those days that will tell you that you have delivered? What are the key currencies that will be used to measure these stops? What position do you expect people (leadership, project team, stakeholders) to be in on those dates?

Quite often on troubled projects, the journey can be hidden under a massive project plan outlining activities without surfacing what the stops in between are and what will you have when you arrive there.

Recap and actions

Essence of this section:

- Understand and uncover if your project has a journey laid out. In specific, check for

- a start (I advise not spending too much time figuring this out apart from the initial conversation to get a bit of context)

- an end (a go-live date and a date for project closeout). The more airy-fairy this is, the more likely that it doesn't exist yet.

- stops in between. Are they visible and clearly articulated? Are they supported by what you will have at those stops, what you will be able to do on those dates and how the relevant people will feel when you reach those stops?

To do:

1   List the responses you get upon inquiry to the questions about the story.

2   Determine whether they are clear or ambiguous.

3   Check this across a section of people on the project.

To *not* do:

- Do not create a new journey immediately.

- Do not try to find fault with people for not having a story.

- Do not dwell too much about why a journey doesn't exist for the project.

One must-read

- Project Management Institute article 'Planning for program closeout' which is about how NASA planned to execute the closeout of America's Space Shuttle Program.[1] (*https://www.pmi.org/learning/library/planning-program-closeout-5844*)

1.3   People who care

Colin D Ellis, in his book 'The Project Book' [1] writes that projects are a result of the person that leads them and the environment they create.'

There are various groups of people involved in projects. Let's explore these groups in some detail.

Leadership

The sun rises every day and infuses energy in us to wake up and do something. Even on rainy, cloudy days, it is almost inevitable that the sun will show up, even briefly to give us that dose of energy.

And then, you have a leaf floating on a stream of water – the stream pushes everything along and the leaf just gets pushed as well.

Coming back to your project, have you ever asked yourself the question – Am I the sun or the leaf?

This can be a critical moment in your project as you stand in front of the mirror and ask yourself this question.

Our journey through the CONFESS stage of rescuing troubled projects is all about facing the mirror and having honest conversations: some with ourselves, some with others.

In this section, we will unpack the leadership or sponsorship aspect of your project. After all, this project starts with the person who leads it. Are you in an appropriate position to lead or sponsor this project?

An effective way to assess this could be based on two factors:

- **Personal investment –** How invested are you in the project outcomes and, by association, the business outcomes? Bear in mind, business outcomes are different to project outcomes and two key failings I see in my experience of troubled projects are

- sponsors are invested in the business outcomes but not necessarily the project outcomes. For example, the head of HR in an organisation absolutely believes in empowering a high-performing workforce through creation of psychological safety and placement of higher responsibility with team members, but doesn't necessarily believe that their human resource information system (HRIS) replacement is the best way to go about it. As a result, this sponsor becomes less invested in the success of their HRIS project and this could be detrimental to that project.

- sponsors confuse one for the other and get caught in the trap of focusing their energies on the wrong things. For example, executives on ERP projects get caught up with technology and features within the software while losing sight of what the ERP is supposed to enable and for whom. I was once involved in an HRIS implementation for a diverse workforce. When I walked in, the project seemed to be in a bit of trouble and there were still discussions happening about new tools being the avenue to increase employee experience, when the biggest problems their employees seemed to face were the administrative overhead and visibility issues caused by existing HR processes. A sponsor invested in business outcomes with a clear commitment to project outcomes that enables realisation of those business outcomes is gold for any project.

- **Authority or influence** – How much authority do you have to influence the project's success? How well positioned are you to shape appropriate project outcomes?

Low authority or influence

Are you passionate and highly invested in the project outcome, but you have a lack of authority or influence? Business professors C.K. Prahalad and Gary Hamel[2] wrote about an anecdotal experiment with four monkeys who were kept in a room with a pole that had bananas on the top. When the first monkey tried to climb up the pole, it was doused with a pail of water and came squealing down. This happened with the remaining monkeys and none of them attempted to reach for the bananas again. One of the monkeys was then replaced by another who had never been doused with water while trying to reach the bananas. When that monkey tried to take action, it was pulled down by the others, possibly out of fear, a need to protect or just to follow the routine. As time went on, all monkeys were replaced and none of them had been doused in water, but none of them seemed to be keen on taking action to reach the bananas. Relating this story back to your project, ask yourself if you believe you can take action to reach for the bananas or are you likely to be pulled down?

A position of low authority or influence can often lead a passionate and highly invested executive down the path of stress and towards a feeling of resignation. In the book *Beyond Performance 2.0* and a series of research articles on McKinsey.com[4], authors Scott Keller and Bill Schaninger touch on a key point of research about instilling ownership on change journeys. They mention research that shows change programs with governance structures clearly identifying roles and responsibilities are 6.4 times more likely to succeed. Among the roles, there is mention of the executive sponsor and the initiative owner, which, according to me, are the most important roles on any project and more so on a troubled project. This research proves the need for a clear outline of authority and influence and yet often on troubled projects I see sponsors have little authority to shape the direction or set the pace. Ask yourself – Am I banging my head against a strong door where I neither have the keys nor the strength to burst through?

Appropriate authority or influence

Conversely, appropriate authority or influence can go a long way in helping a project sponsor or initiative owner set the pace and direction for the project team to deliver on project outcomes.

Returning to the case of the four monkeys, it is worth wondering what might have happened if the fifth monkey was allowed to try. Would it have changed the scenario in the room?

I believe (sometimes contrary to public opinion) that Auckland Council is one of the best places to get things done. The organisation comprises highly passionate and committed people with relatively clear definitions of roles and responsibilities. I had the privilege of being part of their NewCore programme, leading the data migration and data governance streams. The leadership group members were all personally invested and had appropriate levels of authority to get things done. This provided people like me with the right environment to drive through some really challenging pieces of work under strict timeline pressures, not to mention media scrutiny. There are two things I remember from the project:

- It was the leadership who faced the media through those troubled times, stoically responding to some scathing questions and taking ownership.

- When the programme eventually crossed the finish line, it was no longer a headline-worthy topic and very few people turned up to the press conference that was held to announce its successful completion.

This makes we wonder why sensational topics get reported and thrown around more often than real examples of leadership, collaboration and success... but that's for later.

Returning to your project, ask yourself if you have appropriate personal investment and authority to influence and shape the project. Do you feel like the sun, that will rise every day (even on those cloudy, rainy days) and infuse energy?

Locating your position

Look at the keywords in each quadrant in Figure 2 below. Which ones resonate with you in the context of your project?

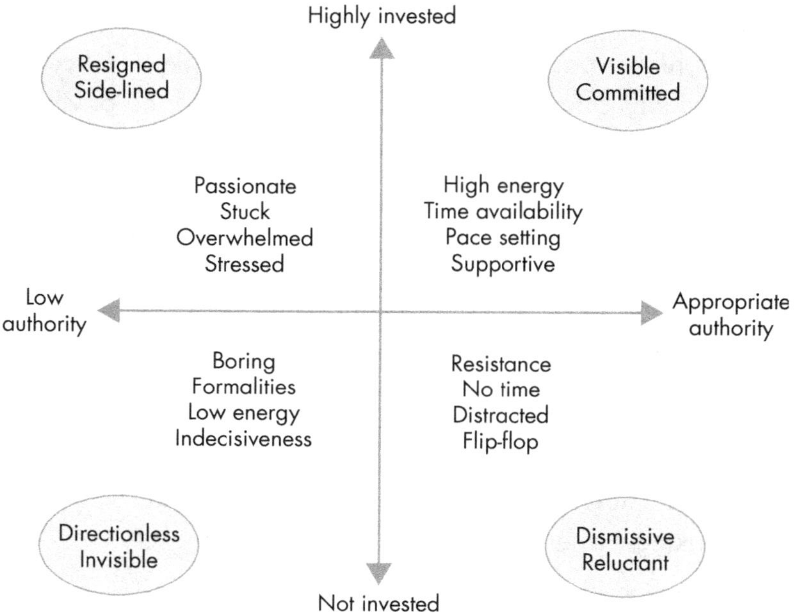

Figure 2.   Project Leadership / Sponsorship – Investment vs authority

At this stage, it is also worth sitting down and having a conversation with your project manager who will need to help you run the next phases. In this conversation, the key things to determine are the suitability of the project manager for the task ahead in terms of their capability, capacity and mind frame.

Quite often, troubled projects take a toll on individuals including the project manager and an exercise you are about to undertake may not be appealing for them to participate in. Have that conversation and decide. Do not go in with someone, who is less than 100% on this journey. Would you fly an aircraft with an exhausted co-pilot?

Recap and actions

Essence of this section:

- Understand your personal investment in the project.

- Understand your authority to drive the project and create the environment.

- Map out where you see yourself on a combination of investment and authority.

To do:

1 Look into the mirror to ask yourself honestly how you are placed to lead this project.

2 Have the same conversation with your project manager.

3 Be light about it. It is not a judgement on you or the project manager. It is about relevance and suitability.

To *not* do:

- Do not make massive changes to the leadership, yet.

- Do not feel disappointed or delusional about your position on the model (remember we are going to change it soon)

- Do not confuse this to be a judgement on you or your project manager as a person. This is about the project and the role you play on it.

One must-read

- The series of five articles from Mckinsey.com summarising the book Beyond Performance 2.0[4] (*https://www.mckinsey. com/business-functions/organization/our-insights/ getting-personal-about-change*)

The team

Have you ever seen a bee colony? I think the metaphor of a buzzing bee colony in a nest or hive is a great way of looking at a project team. Both have a relatively finite lifecycle, a shared purpose, clear roles, even clearer outcomes, and a visible end before they move on to the next nest/project.

When looking at troubled project teams and uncovering what ails them, we need to check the following things.

Appropriate skills

Putting aside the argument that attitude should be the top priority (and it is), would you allow a bunch of your great mates to fly an aeroplane carrying you and your family, if you knew they didn't have the qualifications or experience to fly a plane?

I am hoping you wouldn't. Similarly, on your troubled project, it is worth taking a few moments to note down the names of all your project team members and the skills and expertise they bring. Then ask the following questions:

- Are these skills appropriate for the project this team has undertaken?

- Are the collective skills sufficient for the project journey they have undertaken?

- Do their roles on the project allow/reflect the skills they bring to the table?

Similar to the bee colony, where the queen bee, drones and the worker bees have specific skills[5], a project team needs to have appropriate skills for it to be set up for success.

In the world of projects, skills shortage is often one of the key reasons for project failure.

A Sage Publishing research paper[6] explored the impact of skills shortage on construction projects. Using a sample of 400 construction project practitioners who participated, it was found that unskilled staff had significant negative impact on the project during the construction phase whereas skilled staff had significant positive impact on project performance and enhanced chances of project success.

I think this applies to all projects, especially technology-enabled transformations. Not only am I referring to technical skills but also to other relevant skills like communication, risk management and relationships management.

Stimulating environment

A vibrant and stimulating environment helps create a great project team. Just having the brightest minds (with appropriate skills) will not create a buzzing and motivated team.

In his book, *The Five Dysfunctions of a Team*, Patrick Lencioni[7] outlines five key dysfunctions and all of them point to various aspects of the team's environment. For example, a lack of trust arises from team members not being able to be open, honest and vulnerable with each other; this causes significant challenges in achieving outcomes.

A stimulating environment doesn't just mean you are happy and nice to everyone. A stimulating environment is one where people are allowed to be themselves without having to put on a mask of pretence, and can contribute their best to project outcomes but also understand that free riders and toxic elements are not welcome. Courageous conversations are had openly without fear in a respectful environment[8]. It is an environment where people come in feeling what Amy C. Edmondson refers to as psychological safety in her famous book – *The Fearless Organisation*.

One of the key challenges I often come across while rescuing troubled projects is having to deal with organisations that are undergoing restructuring (or 'right sizing' or 'agile transformation' if you need some jargon attached to it) at the same time. Looking from the outside in, you can clearly see the toxicity, uncertainty and anxiety that exists in such situations and I pity the project environment in such circumstances. If I had my way, I wouldn't do both of them at full speed at the same time.

Returning to your project, the questions worth asking at this stage in terms of environment are:

- Do you see a lot of productive conversations happening on your project within and outside the team? OR

- Do you see a lot of people with headphones on, sunk deep into their machines, or do you see conversations among people?

- Are conversations focused on who people are or what could be done?

- Do you have team members coming up to you often with honest views about their take on the state of things and situations, or do you hear these as rumours?

- Finally, does your team live in a state of fear and withdrawal or energy and openness?

Shared purpose

A shared purpose binds a team together on any project. Projects by nature are a journey into uncertainty and ambiguity. To describe projects, I would use the word *paywat* from the rich Indian language of Marathi – translating to 'the road created by footsteps'.

One of the things I recall from my childhood in a village in Pune, India, was the joy of charting my own path down to the river from my home in the monsoon season. It gave me a great thrill to gather a bunch of mates, roll up our sleeves and shorts and venture into the buzzing rain to find our way to the once beautiful Mula River and then find a small swimming hole. We couldn't afford to go to a swimming pool back then, so this was our best way to swim.

There was no road to reach the waterhole, and any track we made with our footsteps was quickly erased by the rain. Now who could imagine creating a new road to a waterhole almost every day? It was only possible because our enjoyment of swimming in the waterhole, in the rain, was a shared purpose that unified us, day after day. And for that, if we needed to get messy, have a few falls or create our own road, it was worth it.

On a project, a shared purpose is what will keep the team together. Sure, processes, structures, frameworks and methodologies all have a part and rightfully so, but, in times of trouble, a shared purpose is what keeps a project team from disintegrating.

I once led an HRIS implementation at Auckland Council, the largest local government agency in New Zealand and probably Australasia.

There were quite a few challenges on the project but one thing that stood out for me was the shared purpose that bound the team together: the purpose was to make the workforce's HR and HR admin tasks easier and faster. Such a simple yet powerful purpose held that team together through some testing times when it could have been easy to disintegrate.

Does a shared purpose exist for your project? Do people understand and buy into the purpose that this project will deliver? Can you articulate the purpose in a simple sentence without the use of jargon? Is it something every team member of the project will identify with?

If, at this stage of your project, you do not have a clear purpose that is shared by the people associated with the project, do note it down.

This is one of the things we will address as part of the ACT phase and is key to rescuing a troubled project and delivering it successfully.

Recap and actions

Essence of this section:

- Understand if your project team has appropriate skills that collectively fulfil the need to deliver the project.

- Observe and validate if a stimulating environment exists on the project.

- Note if a shared purpose is present and has buy-in from the team.

To do:

1   List team members' skills as accurately as possible.

2   Seek inputs from the team to improve the environment.

3   Check for simplicity and clarity in the shared purpose.

To *not* do:

- Do not go on a hiring spree.

- Do not make massive changes to the environment (counterproductive and confusing).

- Do not immediately hire a consulting firm to find your purpose.

One must-watch

- *A World without Bees* video on the History Channel[9] (YouTube link: *https://www.youtube.com/watch?v=7X1xllyZw3M*)

The stakeholders

Imagine you are an organiser of an international game at Eden Park, the multipurpose sports stadium in Auckland, New Zealand. (It could be any stadium in the world, but I live in NZ and I love Eden Park).

To give you a bit of context, Eden Park is located right in the middle of a residential zone.

With a capacity of 50,000 people, every game that is sold out (and most international games are) means a lot of people, traffic, noise and interruption to residents.

Now, does that mean we stop organising games at Eden Park? Sport is a big crowd-puller in New Zealand and a source of livelihood for many people, including the players themselves. As such, the economic impact of such a decision is quite significant.

Precisely for these points outlined above, there is a well-structured process that involves engagement with all the relevant stakeholders including residents, local government organisations and fans to make choices about which games will go ahead and how to manage the disruption to local residents' lives.

Returning to your project, does it feel similar to organising a game at Eden Park? Where do you see your stakeholders sitting – are they like the residents who are wary of disruption, or the police who need to provide adequate security, or the public transport authority who needs to prepare for the sudden spike of people using trains to get to the venue?

Or are they like the ultimate stakeholder – the fans – who will throng the stadium for the game but leave disgruntled if their experience is not up to standard?

Do stakeholders on your project exist in peaceful coexistence or are there elements feeling short-changed or given the wrong end of the so-called stick?

Balancing stakeholders is a challenge on any project. However, it becomes even more challenging on troubled projects.

The three key words below help to analyse how your project stakeholders are positioned.

- **Identified** – Have you identified the appropriate stakeholders?

- **Represented** – How are they represented on your project?

- **Engaged** – How are they engaged with you on your project?

Let us look at these in some more detail.

Identified

You can only interact with engaged stakeholders if you have identified them consciously. A good starting point is to look at the governance forums and stakeholder identification document (if that exists) to see if you have identified the relevant groups that could impact, or are impacted by, your project.

Take the case of the Millennium Dome[10] project in the UK. The Dome was set up to commemorate the coming of the new millennium. What started as a small project suddenly became large with a change in governments and, at one point, the English public expected a mega structure with wonderful exhibitions. There was also a plan to have a soccer team use it as their home ground, but that didn't materialise. Heavily funded and driven by politicians, the structure failed to attract visitors beyond its initial hype upon opening, and ongoing maintenance cost taxpayers GBP 1 million per month.

While a lot has been said about the planning, financial management and project management of this project, I see stakeholder identification (or lack of) as a key reason for its dire situation. It was predicted to have 12 million visitors a year and about half of that number turned up in the first year. The football clubs which were to call this home never materialised as they never had any involvement or purpose to do so.

Asking the following questions will help you get a better understanding of your project stakeholders.

No.	Question	Yes	No	Maybe
1	Has stakeholder identification been done in a conscious manner?			
2	Have we gone beyond who we know?			
3	Have we identified all possible stakeholders even if their involvement on the project is minimal?			
4	Have we interacted with key people within these stakeholder groups to understand their influence and interest?			
5	Do stakeholders know they are on our list?			
6	Do we have a view of impact on our identified stakeholders?			
7	Does the stakeholder identification exercise include people who may not necessarily be supportive of our project but have significant influence on it?			
8	Is the project leadership (sponsor and project manager/leads) aware of all the identified stakeholders and their relationship (impact/influence) to the project?			
9	Is stakeholder identification an ongoing exercise on the project?			

If the answer to two or more of these questions is *no* or *maybe*, that should tell you a story about your stakeholder identification.

While all the questions above are relevant and important to understand stakeholder identification on your project, special emphasis should be placed on questions 5–9 as they really show you how effective your identification has been.

Represented

Having completed the stakeholder identification assessment, it is important to understand the representation they have on the project. Representation is often a misunderstood and sometimes challenging aspect of stakeholder management. The balance between under- and over-representation is always a tricky one to navigate especially if your project spans across business functions and processes.

Any HCM payroll project is a classic example. The list of stakeholders is diverse and spans the entire organisation. Representing the stakeholders on the project can often be a challenge that could de-rail or dilute project effectiveness.

Let's do an exercise to help you see how well your stakeholders are represented.

No.	Question	Yes	No	Maybe
1	Does the representation of stakeholders trace back to identification?			
2	Does the representation adequately reflect the impact they carry for the project?			
3	Does the representation factor in for influence that certain groups may have?			
4	Does the representation cover groups that could act as gatekeepers when it comes to your project journey?			
5	There is no obvious over or under representation of any particular group.			

No.	Question	Yes	No	Maybe
6	Do we feel there is over-representation for certain stakeholder groups?			
7	Does the representation come across as equitable and balanced?			

If the answer to two or more of these questions is *no* or *maybe*, you might have uncovered another gem on your journey to getting your project back on track. Be happy you've identified something to fix – keep collecting these gems.

Engaged

The third aspect pertaining to stakeholders is engagement. Consider a magnet placed in the midst of iron pieces. With adequate proximity and strength, it attracts most of the iron pieces and keeps them close. The thing to note here is that the magnet draws the iron pieces towards it, rather than the other way round. This is a subtle distinction and nowhere is it more relevant and important than stakeholder engagement. Engaging with your stakeholders is different to getting your stakeholders to engage with you. On a troubled project, it is this part that stands out in the face of challenging situations.

In the summer of 2019, prior to the advent of COVID-19, two separate music concerts were held in Auckland. Two established Bollywood playback singers performed. Both were established legends in the industry with some great hit songs to their credit. I happened to attend both and saw a stark difference in the audience (in both numbers and energy).

While the first was brimming with people in extremely high spirits and energy, the other concert was scrambling for people, even offering tickets for free up to the last moment in a bid to fill up the auditorium. This was further evident in the energy and response of the crowd to the music.

One was top notch while the other was a drag.

So what was the difference? To get an answer to this, I thought back to the months leading up to their respective concerts. For the first one, I could recall almost every place (radio, posters, flyers, social media) that I saw an invitation for this event. It didn't stop at that, there were live radio events, contests, meet-and-greet sessions and a whole raft of other activities where I not only felt represented, but also engaged. The key distinction was, I instantly seemed to recollect almost every interaction I had in the run up to the concert. I participated in some contests, tuned in to certain updates and got the tickets at an appropriate time and they sold out well before the concert day arrived.

For the second concert, all I recalled was seeing a few posters in stores and hearing a couple of mentions on the radio. When I checked for tickets at a very late stage, purely by coincidence, there were still plenty available.

This brings me to the question – Are your stakeholders engaging with your project?

Here are a list of questions that would be worth asking as you unpack the current engagement on your project.

No.	Question	Yes	No	Maybe
1	Do your stakeholders reach out to project team members actively?			
2	Are your stakeholder meetings or engagement points well attended?			
3	Are your stakeholder engagement forums planned and regular?			

No.	Question	Yes	No	Maybe
4	Do you see active participation in the engagement sessions?			
5	Do most of your participants interact actively?			
6	Are there a select few who seem extremely interested in your project?			
7	Do you hold your stakeholder engagement activities on time?			

If the answer to two or more of these questions is *no* or *maybe*, you most likely have an engagement opportunity up your sleeve as well.

Completing this section and its activities should give you some great insights into your stakeholder situation. We will go deeper into those aspects in our ACT, RESOLVE and EXECUTE sections.

For now, give yourself and your team a pat on the back and engage in a mini celebration even if it is just morning tea where each person brings something to the table. Acknowledge the effort and contribution from team members.

Recap and actions

Essence of this section:

- Understanding your stakeholder engagement on a troubled project requires an assessment of

- identification

- representation

- engagement.

To do:

1   Complete the questionnaires about your stakeholders.

2   Be honest about their representation, engagement and influence.

3   Jot down any missing stakeholders that may come to light as you go through these exercises.

To *not* do:

• Do not go on a stakeholder onboarding spree (remember your project is in trouble and they may not be interested [yet]).

• Change governance forums or people within those forums.

• Embark on a massive communication exercise with existing stakeholders (you still do not have a plan to rescue and rebuild confidence).

One must-read

• 'How Gap Inc. Engaged with its Stakeholders' (*MIT Sloan Management Review*)[11] *https://sloanreview.mit.edu/article/ how-gap-inc-engaged-with-its-stakeholders/*

Suppliers

The final big group of people on projects – suppliers – is an interesting one. The reason I say interesting is because this is the group we engage to augment capability and capacity that does not exist or is limited within our organisation.

Quite often the kind of work done by suppliers involves high expertise and is relatively unknown for the groups we discussed previously. This makes it a challenge right at the outset on how we engage and collaborate with this group. It is worth remembering that this group also happens to be the biggest spend bucket on most technology-enabled transformation projects.

We want our relationship with our suppliers to be a long-lasting marriage, and not a bitter divorce, so it's worth setting up a successful partnership by understanding if the following are in place:

- **Accountability**, or 'skin in the game' as it is commonly called. Without accountability, it's just best endeavours – we are friends until I find another.

- **Incentive/reward**. Suppliers need to be incentivised appropriately for them to be set up to deliver.

Equally important, but often only clear once a supplier is on board:

- **Environment** – creating the right environment leads to flowering partnerships.

Let us now look at each of these in a bit more detail and explore how we are positioned with our supplier relationships on the project at this stage.

Environment

Given you are some way through your project at this stage, it is worth starting with the environment. The best indicator of a great project environment is when you cannot differentiate between a person from your supplier organisation and a person from your organisation; they come across as another person within your organisation.

The article 'A winning partnership: Financial institutions and strategic suppliers' published on McKinsey.com[12] refers to the financial services industry and strategic suppliers. While the article focuses majorly on the proportion of services that are outsourced to suppliers, and hence the need for partnership, there is one section on 'the cycle of collaboration'. This section uses the metaphor of a staircase to take supplier relationships to the next level. It talks about starting with the basics of supplier performance and moving up the steps to joint and collaborative innovation. Towards the end of the section, it refers to key parameters that for me represent a good environment in a project – a high level of trust, two-way dialogue, relevant capabilities, fully cross-functional teams and strong performance.

The NewCore programme at Auckland Council is an interesting case in point. This was a programme established to consolidate all the regulatory processes across the erstwhile local councils into the merged Auckland Council entity. The programme was reviewed midway and the budget revised from went up from 71 million to 155 million New Zealand dollars[13].

I had the privilege of being involved in the programme after the reset. I was still working with KPMG New Zealand back then and was called to lead the data migration stream. Data migration on this programme was no mean feat as it involved millions of data records pertaining to regulatory requirements from several disparate systems and applications. I was to lead a team of contractors and a big team of Deloitte consultants, Deloitte having been chosen as the strategic partner to deliver data migration.

Apprehensive as I was, it remains, to date, one of my most memorable and successful projects in the data space. One key hallmark of that team was that beyond the initial few weeks, it was difficult to tell a team member's organisational entity on the project. I reckon that is the kind of environment you want on a project.

Complete the questions below to ascertain characteristics of the environment on your project for your suppliers (partners).

No.	Question	Yes	No	Maybe
1	Do you often hear references to supplier organisations when communicating with your organisational project team members?			
2	Do you often hear references to supplier organisations when communicating with other supplier team members?			
3	Is your team structured by supplier organisations?			
4	Do you often deal with escalations from supplier representatives centred around lack of cooperation?			
5	Do you see long emails which sound like a legal contract for every small decision you are asked to make?			

If you answered *yes* to more than two of the above questions, it is an indication that the environment is not quite right to enable a thriving partnership.

In doing all of this, it would be great if your supplier's people are able to contribute and have conversations on their perspective of the situation. This obviously is more difficult if you are in a legal tussle already and you may need to tread carefully.

Accountability

Accountability helps set expectations and lifts engagement from the levels of just 'best endeavours'.

In late 2018 and early 2019, two Boeing 737 MAX aircraft carrying a combined total of 346 passengers crashed, killing all onboard. The ill-fated flights Lion Air Flight 0610 and Ethiopian Airlines Flight 302 were flying one of the latest, most technologically advanced and sophisticated jets that existed in aviation history. The aviation industry, in spite of the crashes that garner a huge amount of attention, remains the safest mode of transport across the globe. The industry prides itself on its safety record and technological advancements that enhance passenger comfort while continuing to boost safety.

It is very rare to hear of two significant crashes to the same type of aircraft within a span of months. This obviously caught the attention of regulatory officials, media and governments across the world. You can imagine the grief experienced by the near and dear ones of those who perished in the crashes.

In the aftermath, countries across the world grounded the 737 MAX jets and extensive enquiries followed. The investigation narrowed the cause down to the Maneuvering Characteristics Augmentation System (MCAS), which was identified as a factor in both crashes.

What was shocking to note was that neither aircraft revealed any evidence of non-compliance. Yet they were fatally flawed and unsafe to fly. How could that have happened?

The Washington Post[14] revealed that this was in part due to the pressure to get the new planes to customers quickly, without requiring pilots to undergo extensive retraining. The final report highlighted numerous oversight lapses and accountability gaps by the Federal Aviation Authority and its role in both the deadly crashes. And we are talking about an industry that prides itself on its safety record.

The point I try to make here is that, on a project, without accountability, you are just ticking a set of checklists that in themselves may be grossly inadequate and, worse, completely misleading. Sure, the results of a failed ERP or CRM project may not be as bad as losing lives in an air crash but they can still have a massive impact, such as threatening the very existence of the organisation undertaking the project.

I have heard of several transformations that have gone southward resulting in nasty litigations and court battles. Henrico Dolfing, in his book on project failure case studies, refers to a number of such projects that ended up in the courtroom. From National Grid's failed SAP implementation to the massive GBP 10 billion disaster in the UK's National Health Service[15], they were all fraught with supplier accountability issues among others and these played a key role in eventually causing failure or massive pain to the organisations involved.

A clear sign of missing accountability is when you must keep referring to the contracts to see if the supplier is meeting their obligations or not. The moment a contract takes centre stage over collaboration, you have a troubled supplier relationship.

It is like a marriage contract. After marriage, you only take a closer look when you are contemplating divorce!

So, is your supplier relationship bordering on divorce? How is your supplier relationship impacting your project? Is it the cause of trouble on your project? Discuss this with your project manager and key organisational team members.

Also have consultations with your supplier account representative or lead. Having this conversation with your supplier gives them the signal that you are interested in listening and this in turn evokes honest responses.

Whatever the findings, note them down. You have got one side of the supplier relationship analysis sorted with this.

Incentives and rewards

Fixed price! I loathe this term when it comes to complex technology-enabled transformations, yet I see client organisations brandish it as a key achievement – for them it portrays how they have got the best price from a supplier and how it is significantly cheaper than the market rate.

I see organisations focus on getting a fixed price from suppliers, and then impose significant terms and conditions as a prerequisite to be able to have the privilege of doing business.

These organisations don't realise that suppliers need to be incentivised and rewarded appropriately for the accountability they are expected to carry. The balance must be present and visible to the supplier.

Without this, you get a second- or third-rank team of the supplier with little or no interest in delivering the objectives of your project; they will remain compliant, but not collaborative.

On a troubled project, these types of contracts can be a massive drain on time and energy.

Key indications of an incorrect balance between accountability and reward include reduced supplier personnel on the project, regular escalations, constant change requests and a huge administrative overhead when it comes to obligations.

If you see all of these on your project, it is very likely your incentives are not matched to the supplier's accountability, and this is worth noting. It is also worth having a conversation with the supplier on what they think of the model, having been involved in the project for some time. You do not necessarily have to suddenly offer a big rise or shift in the model, but it is worth understanding their view.

Even without a fixed price contract, the incentive for a supplier could be insufficient for the accountability being placed on them. For example, if you have a multi-vendor situation and you essentially hire for named staff on a day-rate basis, the supplier organisation is less likely to be interested in driving overall outcomes for the project beyond providing the named resource and ensuring basic compliance.

Finally, it is worth looking at the offers of suppliers you did not choose at the outset and noting the difference in price and terms between them and the supplier you chose. What this gives you is a view of some of the assumptions made around delivery and informs you if they are still appropriate or not.

Another insight you get from this is whether there was obvious price discounting to land the account. This often happens with smaller firms who heavily discount on price to land the reference client without qualifying the opportunity. Once they get in, they realise they have bitten more than they can chew and the remainder of their journey on the project has painful consequences.

After completing this section, give yourself and the team a pat on the back because going through these conversations to uncover the situation requires courage and honesty. You will use this information in the ACT phase to help structure your project for success (that is, if you choose to go ahead with recovery).

Recap and actions

Essence of this section:

- Understanding your supplier (partner) relationships on a troubled project requires an assessment of

- environment

- accountability

- incentive.

To do:

1 Critically assess your supplier relationships based on the three factors above. Do understand contractual obligations.

2 Include conversations with your suppliers to ensure a balanced view.

3 Note down key findings including anecdotal quotes you may get during the process.

To *not* do:

- Do not get into arguments on contractual obligations or accountability as a tool to get work done.

- Do not suddenly terminate or change the construct of contracts.

- Do not take everything the supplier says at face value. A sense of judgement is needed to balance out the views.

One must-read

- 'A winning partnership: Financial institutions and strategic suppliers' published on McKinsey.com, which is about winning partnerships in the financial sector and provides some good insights on leveraging the potential of suppliers.[12] *https://www.mckinsey.com/industries/financial-services/ our-insights/a-winning-partnership-financial-institutions-and- strategic-suppliers*

1.4   Connections that click

Now that you have looked at the people in your project, it is time to analyse the connections between them.

This is a story about four people named Everybody, Somebody, Anybody and Nobody. There was an important job to do and Everybody was asked to do it. Everybody was sure Somebody would do it. Anybody could have done it, but Nobody did it. Somebody got angry because it was Everybody's job. Everybody thought Anybody would do it, but Nobody realized that Everybody would not do it. It ended up that Everybody blamed Somebody when Nobody did what Anybody could have done.

Have you come across this play of words at some point? It's funny unless you've been in a situation where there was no accountability, in which case it's not so funny anymore.

We've briefly explored the importance of accountability in the previous section, and in this section we'll look at how to identify and improve accountability and governance within a project. Start by asking yourself the following questions.

- In your project, do you often find yourself in long and pointless meetings with people on a topic that doesn't seem to go anywhere?

- Do you sense the lack of pace in decision making impacting your project? Do you always come out of meetings with more questions and actions than decisions?

- Do you find that people turn up to meetings or workshops with little or no preparation and then derail the agenda with off-topic questions?

- Do you see individuals unable to take charge of their activities or to display a sense of ownership?

- Do you walk into steering committee meetings and find yourself discussing technology features at length or walk into architecture boards and find them talking organisation strategy?

If any answers are *yes*, this points to a clear gap in accountability.

To address this, examine the following pillars.

Expertise

If you are not a licensed electrician, do you venture into wiring up a hot water cylinder just because you own your house and you feel you can do it by glancing through content online? On the other hand, do you call for an electrician every time you need to switch on the lights?

No – because you are aware of what requires electrical expertise.

Do you have the right expertise in the room to discuss a particular topic? If the answer is yes, then one of the pillars of accountability and governance is on firm footing and you can move on to the next. If the answer is no, then you already know that you have a gap (or an opportunity to fix this).

Empathy

Have you ever dealt with lawyers or real estate agents? Did you get a sense of being a transaction for them, where their only interest was to move you along like goods on a conveyor belt?

Have you met Owen Aerenga or Andrew Shorthall?

Bear with me. Owen is a real estate agent and Andrew is a lawyer and I had the pleasure of dealing with them both personally when purchasing my house.

Aside from being extremely capable in their areas of work (expertise), they both had something which made me feel that I would love to sit down with these guys and have a conversation. They seemed to understand my family's needs, and the transactions felt easy, comfortable and almost joyful. What they were displaying was empathy, and that made our connection click.

You can use empathy to help you in structuring accountability and governance. Empathy allows you to structure accountability accurately. When you understand what people in various roles see, think, feel, say and do, you get clarity in structuring accountability that works; accountability that feels like a privilege and not a burden to shoulder.

In your current project structure, is there a genuine intent to understand your people before prescribing accountability?

Empowerment

Empowerment has two sides to it – authority and consequence. Authority without consequence could lead to rash decisions and consequence without authority could lead to decision paralysis.

I am a huge cricket fan, so please indulge me and let me tell you the story of the English One Day International cricket team between 2015 and 2019. After their 2015 World Cup quest ended in misery, the team was seen as a failure. Instead of giving up hope, they decided to change the script. The team installed new leadership under a new captain and coach, and invested in a bunch of exciting new cricketeers who were playing a bold version of the game. In 2019 they won the World Cricket Cup (with a bit of luck against us Kiwis). The team was empowered to make huge decisions to strengthen themselves and gain confidence in their own style instead of pressing on with the status quo.

But a moment in their journey stands out. Just weeks out from the start of their World Cup campaign, they decided to drop Alex Hales from their 15-man squad[1]. Alex had set himself up very nicely as a backup option for the preferred opening batsmen – Jonny Bairstow and Jason Roy – but here he was, stood down from the team due to recreational drug use.

The team's messaging was clear – this was not to be the end of Alex's cricket career. They would support him to fulfil his potential as a player.

This illustrated to me that Alex Hales had made a personal choice (authority) to take recreational drugs, for which he had to face being stood down from the team at a crucial moment (consequence).

Does this sort of empowerment exist in your current project?

- Do people have the authority to make decisions or take action that is needed to take the project towards its stated outcome?

- Do people have the psychological safety of being open and honest about failures, learning and challenges?

- Do people on the project have the support that will help them bounce back from failures?

- Do they understand that empowerment comes with consequences (two sides of the same coin) and is there clarity about that?

If you have answered *no* to one or more of these questions, there may be an opportunity to improve the empowerment of your people.

Recap and actions

Essence of this section:

- Understand and uncover if accountability sits nicely and clearly within your project. Key areas to explore are

    - expertise

- empathy

- empowerment.

To do:

1 Perform an honest assessment of where the project sits against these pillars of accountability.

2 Have conversations with project team members to validate your view.

3 Identify areas that may need working through as part of recovery.

To *not* do:

- Do not go on a hiring spree yet!

- Do not suddenly chop and change accountability levels.

- Do not suddenly go a firing spree (unless of course you have an obvious rotten apple on your team).

One must-read

- 'The journey to an agile organization at Zalando' published on McKinsey.com[2] *https://www.mckinsey. com/business-functions/organization/our-insights/ the-journey-to-an-agile-organization-at-zalando*

1.5   The money we need

We are nearly at the end of the confess phase and before we move to the money aspect, it is worth revisiting the business case for the project investment.

A good business case starts with the *'why'*, articulating problems we set out to solve and the reason they matter. It then moves to what this means and how we plan to execute, finally closing off with how we will measure success during and after the project delivery.

Quite often with troubled projects, the leadership gets obsessed with the 'what' and keep pouring money into the project till it is too late. Before you embark on assessing the money situation on your project, it is worth reviewing if the 'why' of the business case still makes sense.

We never have enough money! Most often at this stage on troubled projects, there is a temptation to find more money to try and salvage the downward spiral. But the fact is, the more you focus on consumption, the more the pot dwindles. Another common incidence is that by the time you start uncovering signs of trouble, the allocated money seems to have vanished or is rapidly vanishing.

So how do you take hold of this situation and avoid the downward spiral?

Projects are effective when budgets are secured and governed. A secured budget is a vote of faith in a project and appropriate governance on that budget validates that faith.

On the journey to reviving (or elegantly killing) your project, it is key for you to look at the money from two aspects:

- Is it secured?

- Is it governed?

Let us explore these in more detail.

Secured

Credit card money is money you do not have, and spending money you do not have is going to land you in trouble sooner rather than later. Organisations do not use credit to fund their projects.

Unless there has been some extremely sophisticated algorithm applied to your project funding, you generally know the number that has been allocated to your project. To keep it clean and simple, I would advise looking at the number before contingency is added. I believe contingency, whether it is for known or unknown risks, starts to tread into the territory of 'money you do not have' and can give you a false sense of comfort.

I once worked on a project where the business case included funding that would be made available to the project during its lifecycle due to money saved from operations by reducing headcount. This is what I call wishful thinking. The headcounts never reduced, and the funding never appeared. The result was stress, emotion and scarcity.

The allocated budget or funding is generally available in your approved business case. You may be in a bit of trouble if your project didn't have an approved business case of some sort before you started. I haven't seen a book yet that addresses this problem and I sincerely hope your project is not a reason to write a book on recovering projects that were started without a business case.

Note down the budget that was allocated to your project. This is what I call 'the money you had'.

The next data point to look at is the money spent to date. In most cases, you will have a project code in your finance system that helps you capture all the spend to date. A summary of this should give you your spend to date.

The remainder, of course, is the money you are left with (real money, I mean).

There is one more aspect to project budget and that is your own people's time. This is often a second trap projects fall into. Projects, especially technology-enabled transformation ones, have a significant amount of time investment expected from people within the organisation to make them a success.

Unless a particular person is seconded to the project, they generally make do with contributing a portion of their time to the project, while balancing the responsibilities of their day job at the same time. This is a contentious area and I liken it to the first few days after a baby arrives in your family: sleepless nights become the norm for a period of time, but you still have to turn up to work and be effective.

Some organisations and projects manage this better than others but, in general, this is a trouble area when it comes to project funding.

Now, while this may not seem like 'real money' to come out of your budget (unless you are going to hire a temporary person to backfill a project contributor) it is worth noting that there is an expectation from people to allocate time for the project, and this time is critical to allow external partners to deliver their commitments.

To give you a good sense of where you are with people's time on the project, I would suggest you note down the time forecast you had outlined for all the organisational staff on the project. If you have a project management system, you should also be able to get a view of actual time that has been invested to date. If you do not have a project management system, it is worth checking with all the project contributors on how much they actually spend on the project in any given week.

A summation of this should give you a reasonably accurate picture of time spent so far. It also gives you a picture of time you have remaining.

With this, you have two key pieces of data:

- Money you have remaining (secured) to spend on the project.
- Time you have remaining (hopefully secured) to spend on the project.

I am hoping the figures you have for both of these are not in the negative or close to zero.

Before we move on, there is one more thing I would advise you to jot down: the assumptions you made in the business case while making the case for funding. These assumptions are one of the most powerful tools we have on projects that are essentially a venture into uncertainty.

On a piece of paper, or a PowerPoint slide, note down all the assumptions (verbatim) from your business case. You may have made some more assumptions during your project journey after the business case and it would be worth including these as well.

Once you have these listed, highlight the ones that have an obvious link to money. If it isn't obvious at first glance, just leave it alone. It is not the end of the world. The key here is to select as many as you can (in say 10 to 15 minutes) that show an obvious direct link to money.

Imagine, for example, you assumed 15 technology integrations (three high-complexity, seven medium-complexity and five low-complexity). If this was one of the assumptions you made, it is likely that you put a dollar amount against integration based on this and that, for me, is an obvious direct link.

Governed

Money is like the fuel in your car. Let us assume that you have chosen the most fuel-efficient car.

If you are a smooth driver and follow a disciplined driving pattern, avoiding abrupt breaking, rapid acceleration and ad hoc speed shifts alongside observing your fuel indicator, you will always have a sense of when the next fuel stop is and how far you can go with the current fuel.

Contrast this by imagining yourself as an absent-minded driver who keeps the air conditioning on with the windows open, doesn't bother looking at the fuel indicator and hasn't any idea where the next fuel station is. You are riding your luck.

The same applies to money on your project. For discussion purposes, we'll restrict ourselves to the money we have secured.

- Do you have governance of funding visible on your project?

- Do you have levels of money spend that can be authorised by various project team members or leads within your project?

- How are necessary changes to work reflected when it comes to funding?

- How do you ensure that the time requested on the project for organisational staff is allocated and consumed through the project?

- How timely do the payable invoices come in and do you know all the spend that is going to hit you every month?

- Do you know of money that goes out regularly like a direct debit?

- Do you know of occurrences of impulse buying (for example, a small piece of software that sounds cheap to help enhance user experience when it wasn't in the original budget) happening on your project and how they are authorised?

- Do you know about payments that have not been made for invoices/expenses that should have been?

If the answer to most of the above is *yes*, then you are reasonably well governed when it comes to money. If not, then you have the opportunity to be so.

With the information you have collected above, you can plot where you stand on our project when it comes to money. The following quadrant (Figure 3) is something I would strongly recommend even if comes across as a bit judgemental. After all, this CONFESS stage is all about laying it out as it is so that we can change it for good.

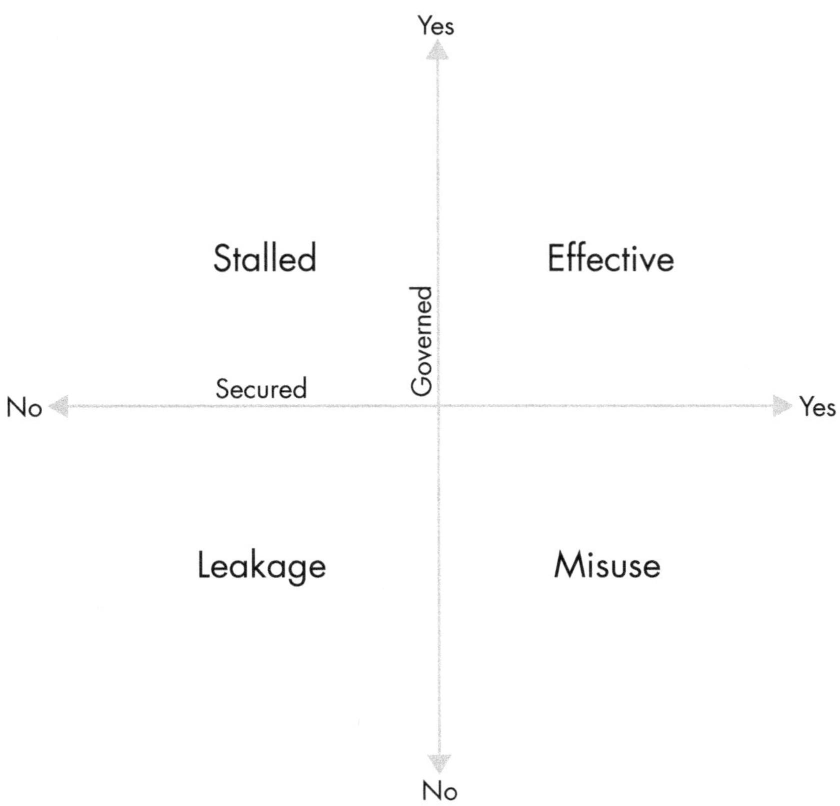

Figure 3. Secured vs governed money on a project

You will most likely find yourself in the 'misuse', 'leakage' or 'stalled' quadrants if you are truly in the midst of a troubled project.

Of these quadrants, I believe the leakage quadrant is the hardest to recover from, followed by the stalled and misuse quadrants. Your aim is to be placed in the effective quadrant. We will address how to get there in the ACT phase.

Recap and actions

Essence of this section:

- Understanding your project budget situation is an important aspect of project recovery.

- Understanding whether your budget is secured and governed will provide good insight into the amount of effort needed to bring the project back on track.

- Having visibility of the remaining budget and remaining time (from organisational staff) on the project will put you in a good place to recover the project.

To do:

1　Collect information on the remaining budget and time as accurately as possible.

2　Critically place your project on one of the quadrants against the axes of secured and governed budgets.

3　Align this information with the finance and HR functions in your organisation.

To *not* do:

- Do not include contingency budgets into this calculation for now.

- Do not include any operations funded budget that is dependent on certain things happening (for example, reduction of operational staff).

- Do not be overly optimistic in assuming people could make more time for the project.

One must-read

- The article 'Elephant on thin ice: Navigating complexity through project culture' published by the Project Management Institute. Focus on the acknowledgment part more than anything else[1]. *https://www.pmi.org/learning/library/ navigating-complexity-project-culture-10181*

1.6   The rules of engagement

Projects offer numerous possibilities. They are a catalyst to non-linear organisational growth. They are the mechanism that allows organisations to make significant shifts on their journey to achieving their mission. Yet like nuclear energy, they can quickly turn dangerous for organisations if they go uncontrolled.

In the world of a project, rife with uncertainty, run by imperfect people, guiding principles (or 'rules of engagement') are the difference between success and failure. Think about nuclear energy released in a nuclear power station generating useful electric energy compared to an uncontrolled nuclear accident.

I use two simple factors to ascertain the influence of guiding principles in any troubled project:

- **Existence** – Do guiding principles exist?

- **Embodiment** – Are these known, understood and utilised to guide your project journey?

Existence

Let's return to the idea of a beehive. A beehive is one of the most marvellous creations in this world. So much natural sweetness is created by a large team that always seems to be working in unison.

The rules governing a hive are interesting to see. The queen bee, workers (females) and drones (males) have clear roles to play and seem to adhere to rules, playing their role to perfection to create successful results. If they didn't follow their internal rules, imagine the chaos and self-destruction inside the hive with bees doing the wrong jobs, getting in each other's way, and accidentally (or purposefully) stinging each other[1].

I think there is a similarity to people on projects. Of course, it is very rare for someone to 'sting' anyone else on a project to the extent of killing them or being killed themselves, but the literal translation of the sting can be seen in the handling of any conflict or effect on our emotions throughout a project's lifecycle.

Do you have guiding principles or rules of engagement on your project?

These should be established upon commencement of a project. They could have a number of aspects including rules of being, saying, doing and thinking (we will explore these in detail during the ACT stage). For now, all we are looking for is whether they exist or not.

It is probably very obvious that ground rules to drive behaviours on projects are essential, but given the enormity of them, sometimes they are not made clear.

A simple guiding principle like 'Adopt not adapt' is so powerful in the world of technology-enabled transformations that are supported by a software as a service (SaaS) application. When faced with a plethora of choices at each step on how the application could be leveraged for business processes, this principle, deployed effectively, can streamline delivery to a significant extent.

Embodiment

The mere existence of guiding principles without embodiment results in ineffectiveness at best.

Some key questions worth asking at this stage to give you a sense of embodiment are shown in the table below.

Question	Yes	No	Maybe
Do conversations or meetings look like a debate that people are trying to win?			
Do decisions often seem inconsistent and scattered?			
Do you see pockets of individuals operating on the project as opposed to in cohesive teams?			
Do you see the messaging and actual work done on the project at odds with each other?			
Do you see people being reserved or very cautious in offering their views/options on the project?			

If you answered *yes* to more than one of the above questions, it is very likely that guiding principles are not embodied within people on the project.

James P. Carse, in his book *Finite and Infinite Games*[2], talks about how a finite game is played to win while an infinite game is played to continue the play, and explains how the rules are formed and followed for each of these. For example, rules in a finite game (say, a soccer game, or a job interview) are formed and everyone plays to those rules to maximise their chance of winning. Finite games are always focused on having a winner. Conversely, an infinite game has rules that can be adjusted as we go to keep playing. For example, during a conversation with your partner, you may notice them getting annoyed and so you adjust your approach to keep the conversation going.

Prof. Carse claims that a number of finite games can be played within an infinite game, but you can never play an infinite game within a finite game.

I think this last statement in the context of projects is extremely relevant. Projects are temporary (yes, temporary could mean a few years) and by definition finite. So they do need to have rules that govern a finite game. However, a project is driven by a set of people who care. They are all playing the project game to win as a project team. Sure, in that process, each one may grow and win differently from an individual perspective but the eventual objective is overall project success. Where you see an embodiment of rules that are played to win against one another on a project, you are flirting with danger.

Equally, a project is part of an infinite game as far as the organisation's and the individual's futures are concerned. For an organisation, this project could mean the difference between staying in business and going belly up. For an individual, a lot may be riding on their career based on this project. So, it is important to ensure we do not forget the infinite game in our quest to narrowly treat the project as a finite game that needs to be 'won' at all costs.

So how do you define guiding principles that allow you to play a finite game (that is, to achieve project success) yet keep us playing happily into the future in the infinite game? We will explore this in the ACT stage.

For now, you need to have a frame of reference on where your project and people sit when it comes to the existence of guiding principles and their embodiment. I would urge you to have a look at the quadrant below (Figure 4) and plot for yourself where people on your project are placed currently. Armed with this knowledge, you can go about putting life back into the project.

To do this, get inputs from your key people on the project and also from others connected to the project to ensure it's not your sole perspective.

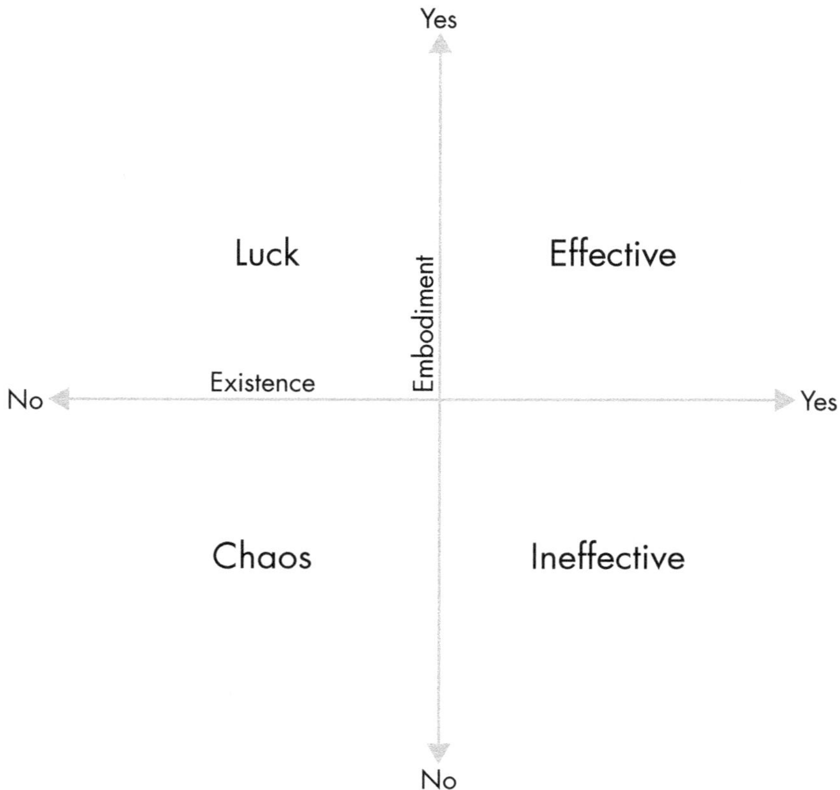

Figure 4.   Existence vs embodiment

The 'luck' and 'chaos' quadrants are the ones to watch out for. If you find your project and its people in these quadrants, your road to recovery is likely to be more challenging, though not impossible.

Recap and actions

You have now mapped out your entire project situation in the CONFESS stage. Well done, give yourself a pat on the back.

We have covered the following:

1   Destination – Do we know about this and does someone care?

2   Journey – Do we have one that makes sense?

3   People – Do we have people who care?

4   Connections – Do we have connections that click?

5   Money we need – Do we have money secured and governed?

6   Guiding principles – Do they exist and are they embodied?

You can now explore the next phase – ACT – in which we'll address any opportunities discovered above to put joy and life back into our project (or even elegantly euthanise it).

Essence of this section:

- In a journey filled with uncertainty and driven by people, guiding principles are key to eventual success (or failure).

- Evaluating the existence of guiding principles is the first step.

- Evaluating embodiment of these principles gives us a good reality check on the project.

To do:

1   Seek inputs from people within the project and those connected to its outcomes.

2   Critically evaluate the existence and embodiment aspects.

3   Lay out where your project stands on the existence vs embodiment scales.

To *not* do:

- Do not judge people or teams based on the evaluation.

- Do not perform the evaluation without anyone else's perspectives.

- Do not suddenly impose a list of rules that create even more havoc on the project.

One must-read

- Finite and Infinite Games by James P Carse.[2]

2

ACT

2.1   A destination worth visiting

Well done on working through the CONFESS phase.

At this stage of your project, you and your project manager are like pilots at the helm of a troubled jet. Systems are failing, alarms are sounding, but you have kept a clear head and you have run through all your checklists to uncover what factors are causing the emergency.

This is great. You have a realistic view of what ails your project, and you have time to recover it before a crash landing is imminent.

For mid-size projects (with teams of 20 to 50 members) the ACT phase should take you between two and four weeks, depending on the scale of your organisation and people's availability to participate.

Like the CONFESS stage, it is appropriate to start with the destination in mind. Whether you are in a corporate, not-for-profit or government organisation, projects must be aligned to the destination the organisation is seeking to reach, taking a set of chosen paths (strategies) decided upon by the leadership. It helps to see strategies as paths chosen to be taken and projects as bridges that are built to navigate the chosen paths as we go.

Are these the only paths? No.

Are they the right paths? Maybe.

Could we take a different path? Possibly.

However, these paths, or strategies, have been chosen after careful consideration, often with the collective wisdom of a group of people. While alternative paths may always be available, it is important to know and stick to remit.

For the purposes of this exercise, let us make an assumption that the strategies have been finalised by the organisation.

If the organisational mission is already in place and strategies to achieve those are also laid out, how do we frame up the context for our project to exist?

In the CONFESS section, we sought answers to:

- Product or service – What will your project deliver?

- Outcomes – What will the product or service enable?

- People – Who will benefit from it and do they care?

You will now take these and work out the context for your project. The easiest place to start is with the project sponsor and/or the leader of the business unit that will benefit the most from this. They may or may not be the same person, depending on the project.

When it comes to defining the drivers or purpose for a project, we are essentially trying to frame up the bridge it builds on the path (strategy) the organisation has chosen to take.

What that bridge is, where it leads and whether it is the right one depends on the organisation and the project. One of the possible outcomes from this phase is that you determine that this project is a bridge to nowhere – and that is OK.

For now, we will focus on defining the bridge. We consider three factors:

- Alignment to strategy and priority

- Delivered product (or service) and alignment to outcomes

- People who care

Alignment to strategy and priority

Every organisation will have a clear business unit (this could be a department or division, or in the agile world a tribe, chapter, squad or gang (hopefully not 😊)) from which this project is driven. The business unit will form part of a broader organisational pillar such as finance, HR or operations.

This organisational pillar will no doubt have a set of strategies to enable certain outcomes for the organisation.

Let us take the HR function in any organisation for example. If one of the organisational outcomes is to enable a high-performance and engaged workforce that will delight their customers, then one of the strategies might be to enable capability that will help this workforce to focus on their core roles.

Now let us assume this organisation has busy staff who currently have to perform all their HR processes manually, from recruiting people to applying for leave manually to delivering printed payslips. It is evident that the capability needed to enable a high-performance workforce is missing. A project to deliver this capability (like an HRIS solution with mobility features such as an app to view your payslip) is a bridge that can lead this organisation to their desired destination.

You will need to find what that is for your project in the context of your organisational strategy. Starting with the project sponsor or the business unit leader will give you a defined frame of reference. In most cases, this will need nothing more than a couple of conversations. Remember there are no right or wrong answers; rather, you will get appropriate answers that make sense for your organisation.

The alignment to strategy is paramount and finding it (if it doesn't exist) for your project will often be one of the most challenging parts of the ACT phase. It's critical to involve key leadership team members in contributing and reviewing the strategy to ensure a successful recovery.

Having articulated how the project relates to strategy, it is then appropriate to review where this project figures in terms of priority against other initiatives.

A leading organisation here in New Zealand embarked on an ERP and HRIS replacement programme. This was established to be critical to strategy at an organisational level. However, when COVID hit, strategies had to be reviewed and prioritised quickly. Overnight the strategies around survival and holding firm took centre stage over ambitious growth plans. A review of all projects and programmes were duly undertaken and it was decided to put the ERP and HRIS programme on hold.

Was the project in trouble? No.

Was it aligned to strategy? Yes.

Was it high up on the priority list given the changing dynamics and resulting strategy? No.

The Project Management Institute (PMI) runs an initiative called the Pulse of the Profession. In 2014, they ran this on the topic 'The high cost of low performance'[1]. This was based on feedback and insights from about 2,500 project management leaders and practitioners across the world. One of the key findings was that less than half (~42%) of organisations report high alignment of projects to organisation strategy.

Read that again – one in two projects are misaligned to organisational strategy.

This explains why so many projects fail to sustain momentum beyond the initial launch days. This also provides insight into the historical success rates of projects which languish around one in three.

The numbers haven't changed much since then!

A question which keeps coming up about projects is if the agile approach could change this. Agile still requires you to have a vision and do the planning before you get launched into delivery. Sure, agile gives you levers to quickly recognise failures/misalignment and course correct, but it still won't fix a project that is fundamentally misaligned to strategy if you continue pursuing it.

It is worth remembering that effort invested in ensuring alignment to strategy for a project is always worth it. Even if the strategy were to change, you know how you could adjust your project to adapt.

People who care

You need to have people who care for the outputs produced by a project, and you need people who will truly benefit from the outcomes your project enables. Without them, the project would run just as a formality.

While we will cover this in better detail in the next chapter, the key exercise here is to ascertain the list of stakeholders (or more specifically, end customers) who would be the recipients of the benefits this project promises.

Take the example of a state-of-the-art HRIS and payroll solution implementation. You might say that implementing this solution benefits everyone across the organisation, but this is too vague. Instead, break it down.

Your first group of stakeholders might be the employees. List a couple of benefits the project will give them (for example, they will get access to an app through which they can apply for leave and view their payslip). Also list a couple of points about how this will impact them (for example, some people may not have a smartphone or want to use an app due to the data usage required). You could rate the benefits and impacts on a scale where 1 is low and 5 is high.

Your next set of stakeholders might be the managers, people leaders or supervisors in your organisation. Repeat the same process with them: find 1–3 benefits and 1–3 areas of impact with a rating between 1 and 5.

Perform this exercise within your core project team until you run out of options. If you do have some engaged stakeholders at this stage, seek their input into this process. People are more than happy to help if you ask and could be the key to unlocking your understanding of the stakeholders.

Once you have done this, select representatives from these people groups across the organisation to validate your end product.

Delivered product (or service) and alignment to outcomes

Every project must deliver a product or a service. That product or service must enable a set of envisaged outcomes. Without these the project is worth junking!

Hans Christian Andersen's short story 'The Emperor's new clothes' is a classic. In it, an emperor is fooled into buying an expensive non-existent outfit, and parades in the nude[2].

It is worth ensuring your project does not turn out to be the emperor's new clothes. Given your project is some way down the track at this stage, you should be able to look at what has been produced to date and get a view of what the end product will look like.

Try running information sessions to share the progress with key stakeholder groups while articulating what it will become by the end of the project.

There are a couple of things to do before running the information sessions:

1   Work with your team to create the experience you want the stakeholders to have during the information sessions. Spend time rehearsing and sharpening your presentation. If you have an already engaged stakeholder, leverage them for feedback. Also take time to run this past the relevant leadership, especially your steering group or the sponsor.

2 Clearly agree on the setup and roles your project team members will play during the session. Depending on the number of stakeholder groups you want to reach out to and the number of repeat sessions, it is worth having more than one person within your core team to back up some roles during the sessions.

In the sessions, seek feedback from stakeholders on the features they need for the product to be complete. It is neither possible nor necessary that you incorporate every feature they ask for, but it is important to understand how far your project deliverables are from that list.

Typically, you would run these sessions with groups of 8–10 people and provide them the opportunity to provide inputs. If your project has decent alignment to strategy, you will find that the core features you have produced (or intend to produce) will resonate and align with your stakeholders. It is the additional ones that may need working through.

This is almost a retrospective validation of business requirements.

One area in which organisations get trapped frequently is a myth around software as a service (or 'plug and play'). In the software applications space, as one of my client CIOs said, the only thing that works in a plug and play mode is Microsoft Word!

Beware of this trap as it can lure you into a misleading sense of confidence that the tool has everything you need.

SAP SuccessFactors, for example, is a leading HRIS solution being implemented by organisations across the world. However, the features it has for management of a contingent or contract workforce (gig workers as opposed to employees) is limited. SAP themselves promote another product called SAP Fieldglass for this requirement.

If your organisation has a large contingent workforce and you went in with the SaaS 'plug and play' mentality, blinded by the application promises, you are likely to be on slippery ground. This is where validating the value of the end product or service with the business will come to your rescue and give you the critical insights you need.

Performing this exercise has another benefit: it starts to give you a sense of the change impact that will need to be managed within your organisation due to the delivery of this project. A great change manager should be across this phase alongside your key project people to ensure you understand the change properly and can plan for it.

Taking the above example of an HRIS solution with mobility features, this exercise should bring out any concerns people have with mobility including access to a smartphone with adequate data packs to use the feature.

This exercise also allows people an opening to start engaging with your project. They begin to have input into the product, and, through feedback sessions, they start to understand the rationale for a certain feature or requirement not being incorporated in the product.

There are two big benefits from doing this exercise:

- You start doing the project *with* people and not *to* people.

- You find out very quickly if your existing output is aligned to what the users expect or not.

With this, you now have the answers to whether this project leads to a destination worth visiting.

You start forming a picture of the following:

- Is the solution fit for purpose?

- The benefit that your stakeholders see and perceive along with its worthiness for them.

- The impact it is likely to have on them as they transition from current state to the future state.

Recap and actions

Essence of this section:

- Validate if your project has a purpose that is worth striving for.

- Alignment to strategy and priority: Does this project align to organisational strategy and produce something of value? Is it a priority right away?

- Outputs aligned to outcomes: What does the project deliver and what outcome does it enable?

- People who care: Who are your key stakeholders (customers) and are they seeing this as a benefit?

To do:

1   Identify the key stakeholder groups and set up information exchange sessions.

2   Create the experience they will be taken through in these sessions.

3   Seek input and feedback to validate the picture you had earlier.

To *not* do:

- Do not justify or be defensive towards any feedback you receive in the information sessions.

- Do not try and address the entire organisation or representatives of groups beyond what is sufficient.

- Do not promise too many things or raise too many expectations that may not be feasible to deliver.

One must-read

Project Failures: London's £1M Per-Month Millennium Dome[3] (*https:// www.brightwork.com/blog/project-failures-londons-1m-per-month-millennium-dome*)

2.2   People who care – Part I

In Chapter 1.3, as part of the CONFESS phase, we looked at various groups of people on your project. In this chapter, we will look at how to improve the engagement of these groups for the project's success.

The project sponsor

The first person we need to enable on the project is you!

As the sponsor, you will have noted the quadrant in which you located yourself in Figure 2 'Investment vs authority':

1   Visible and committed

2   Dismissive and reluctant

3   Directionless and invisible

4   Resigned and side-lined

This section is for those of you who located yourself in quadrants 2 to 4. If you located yourself in Quadrant 1, you may want to skip this section.

So how do we move you as the sponsor to Quadrant 1 to be visible and committed?

Firstly, it's essential at this point to ask yourself whether you *want* to move into Quadrant 1. The answer to this will depend on the following:

- Your level within the organisation in terms of authority and empowerment

- Are you merely supportive of the project or do you and your team stand to gain materially in your roles within the organisation? Does the delivery of this project support your KPIs, your people and how closely it is aligned to organisational strategy?

- How invested you are to drive this home amongst other priorities.

The first bullet can be discussed with your relevant leadership teams. The other two bullets however are ones you must answer for yourself. If you answer *high*, then you are the appropriate sponsor to be the face of this project. If the answers are *low*, then you will need to find another person within your organisation to sponsor or lead the project.

Don't let a feeling of possessiveness over the project cloud your judgement about whether you are the appropriate sponsor. A great project manager is worth their weight in gold in this situation – they can provide advice based on their experience and understanding of organisational context.

Having decided that you are the right person to be visible and committed, we can look at the aspects that enable you to be an effective sponsor and to move yourself into Quadrant 1 on the grid.

Passion

You need passion if you are to sponsor any project. A passionate sponsor truly believes they can make a difference to the organisation through this project.

Without a passionate sponsor, a project is a chore no one wants to do.

Passion provokes you to think deeply and be present when the project requires. It helps you identify the key areas in which you need education or backing, and enables the clarity for you to ask for it.

Colin D Ellis, a reputed thought leader and author in the project management space, has written a book aptly titled *The Project Rots from the Head*[1]. It is all about effective project sponsorship and the importance of it to prevent projects from failing repeatedly. If you get a chance, I recommend having a read.

Time

Yes! If passion is the fuel that sparks the ignition in a car, time is the accelerator that keeps it going.

Pure passion without the commitment of time is like daydreaming – you get inspired by the vision of what this project could do to your organisation, how it would positively impact people's lives and what it could do for your career – but a dream is how it will always remain.

At this point, ask yourself if you have the time to give to this project.

If the answer is *no*, then you need to ask yourself how you will make the time. Not making time is not an option if you passionately believe in the project as a priority.

As much as we speak of agile self-organising teams and the breakdown of hierarchy, a 'present' sponsor who is there in the arena, putting in the time and effort with the team, is the single most important reason why one project will most likely succeed while others around it languish in the doldrums.

The best way to understand the time commitment required is to have a frank conversation with your project manager and align your expectations. You should understand where your time is the most valued from a project perspective, and everything else should be managed by others.

If you accept accountability for the project, you will make time for it. Remember, it takes a lot of commitment to see a project through even if you have a large team at your disposal to do the work.

If you believe you do not have the time, it is worth asking yourself again whether you are the right sponsor for this project or if this project is worth doing right now.

Selectivity

If you have a gruelling schedule and some of your key success metrics are related to projects, it is imperative that you choose the right projects to sponsor.

It is like parenting. It does not stop at birth. Just conceiving a project and leaving it there will not have a good outcome. The need for you to be across the projects you sponsor is critical and the best way to ensure this is to be selective about which ones you sponsor.

To be effective as a sponsor, select the projects in which you are highly invested in the outcome, have the passion for, and can commit time to. For the rest, either try and find another sponsor who could tick the above or prioritise among them to ensure adequate focus.

Project manager

On your project, the first person to consider is your project manager.

Who would you prefer to fly your aircraft – autopilot, or the celebrated US Airlines pilot Captain Chesley Sullenberger[2] (famous for successfully landing a passenger flight in the Hudson River after losing both engines)?

Let me elaborate.

I just searched on SEEK.co.nz for 'Project Manager' roles and found 4,224 ads. Whoa!

That is an amazing number of jobs in a small country like New Zealand.

The following key words were repeated in most of them: *Communication, budget, stakeholder management, attention to detail.*

In a subsequent conversation with an acquaintance who was hiring for project and programme managers, they expressed frustration at not finding any suitable candidates. This got me thinking – if projects are about a journey into uncertainty to fuel your organisation's growth, and they succeed and fail on the work quality of the people involved, then why do you look for autopilots when it comes to picking your project manager?

The keywords in the job ads are generic and will attract autopilots.

When it comes to selecting a great project manager, I generally recommend the following:

- *Comfort with ambiguity* – think of Captain Sullenberger and his emergency landing. Seek project managers who can thrive in ambiguity! Those who can keep their head and make decisions while in trouble and faced with multiple possibilities and choices.

- *Separation* – you cannot see light with your head in the sand. The project manager should have the ability to separate themselves from the problems and solutions while helping the team work through it.

- *Anticipation* – this comes mostly with experience but is often underestimated. The TCAS system in an aircraft alerts pilots to possible collisions, but it takes a pilot to follow one.

A great project manager also adds value by virtue of the scars they carry; that is, the learning they have derived from past failures or complex situations.

If you haven't already made a decision in the CONFESS phase, it is worth considering now if your current project manager fits the bill or not.

Your current project manager may be totally exhausted at this stage of the troubled project, and may not be the right person to undertake the challenge of recovering it.

In this case, as the sponsor, you need to have an honest conversation with them to agree on the best way forward for the project. It may be appropriate to acknowledge their contribution thus far, identify a suitable replacement and begin a smooth transition.

Stakeholders

The moment you do projects *to* people, they do resistance *to* your project!

Replace *to* with *with* and you will see collaboration replacing resistance. This is not just a linguistic distinction. It is fundamental when it comes to project success.

Ultimately your project is done for a group of stakeholders, or customers. It solves a particular pain or enhances a particular experience or helps them make or save money.

In the CONFESS section, we looked at the three key parameters of stakeholder relationships, which are:

- identification

- representation

- engagement.

You should have your findings handy from that exercise. Now we will get to work to improve all of these parameters.

There are three groups of people involved in this next exercise:

- The sponsor

- The project team

- The immediate beneficiary team (in the example of an HRIS implementation, this would be the HR function within the organisation).

Start conversations with the high-level, macro organisational unit leaders who could be key stakeholders. From there work with the project team to zoom in further within those organisational units to identify key people who could represent those units. Start placing them in logical groups of governance mechanisms or connections that you will need to establish for the project to be successful.

Next, approach key people within the immediate beneficiary team to further focus on individuals who could influence or impact the project in a proportion that is greater than their individuality in the organisation.

An article published on McKinsey.com by Bill Schaninger and Taylor Lauricella[3] touched upon this aspect in some detail. It challenged some of the traditional stakeholder identification and management techniques in terms of gaps that exist when it comes to individuals or teams that exert far greater influence than their size when it comes to projects.

The best people to let you know about these influential individuals are members of the immediate beneficiary team as well as your project team who will have crossed paths with some of them on the project journey this far.

Now, having identified these people and people groups, prepare a zoom-in and zoom-out map literally showing how organisational units with specific teams represented by selected individuals would be represented on your project journey. This gives you a good picture of stakeholder representation. Ensure that key managers or people leaders are represented on appropriate governance forums to formalise stakeholder engagement and also make it two-way.

On a project it is not only important to identify, understand and listen to the stakeholders, but it is equally important that they take responsibility and accountability to do their part of the deal. In this case it could be specific people leaders representing a key organisational unit who need to communicate with their team on the upcoming process or technology change that their team members will need to adopt and why. Also important is them lending credibility to the outcomes of the project and ensuring they drive the change in their respective business units through their messaging, personal backing and support.

A great change manager on your project can make this whole activity a breeze while an incompetent one can make it miserable. If your change manager cannot help you through the identification, then you must seriously consider finding a better one.

While we have already discussed stakeholders within your organisation, it is important to now also uncover the ones external to your organisation. In this case, it could be the unions, regulatory authorities, media, auditors, councillors, elected members of parliament or even some external consultants and contractors. You can never be exhaustive enough in your identification and should you decide to continue this project, this is something that will continue to get refined throughout the project lifecycle.

In this ACT phase, you want to have a mechanism that allows you to continually focus on and embed this stakeholder identification within your project delivery and governance. Identifying the governance forums that will facilitate this and the connections people in your project team will ensure you never leave a stakeholder disengaged, or at least you will have done everything required from your side to ensure it is worthwhile.

Once you have identified, represented, and ensured mechanisms for engagement, round it off by communicating your findings with the key representatives and agree on the mutual responsibilities and accountabilities. Leverage the governance groups and leadership meetings to ensure this is effective.

Lay out cadences and contact points for all groups to be able to approach and engage with your project. Leave no stone unturned in getting the composition of key governance groups and leadership teams engaged. At this stage of your project it is not worth going beyond the leadership and key governance groups because you haven't yet made the decision on whether to continue this project or not.

Done well, this can be a hugely satisfying experience and it will start to build some of the foundations of a great project recovery.

Approach this with utmost transparency, a keenness to serve and a true intent to have conversations of value and you will see your stakeholders rediscovering the love.

You will notice that we haven't covered your project team and your partners (suppliers) yet. There is a reason for this, and we will come back to them in Section 2.4: People who care – Part II.

Recap and actions

Essence of this section:

- Work needs to be done with people who care for a project to be successful, starting with the

    - sponsor: the face of the project needs to be visible, committed and engaged

    - project manager

    - stakeholders: all people groups who have influence or could be impacted by your project need to be identified, represented and set up to engage.

To do:

1 Follow the process outlined for each group and focus on the key parameters.

2 Utilise your change manager to help you navigate this.

3 Agree on the benefits and responsibilities making it a mutually beneficial relationship.

To *not* do:

- Do not accord undue influence or power to a particular group resulting in favouritism bias.

- Do not suddenly expand the scope and outcomes to please particular groups to the detriment of the project.

- Do not try to cast every relationship/connection in a formal setup. Some need to be informal and connecting. This means they have to be beyond formal forums. They have to be regular conversations and connections.

One must-read

McKinsey article – A data-backed approach to stakeholder engagement[3] (*https://www.mckinsey.com/business-functions/ organization/our-insights/the-organization-blog/a-data-backed-approach-to-stakeholder-engagement*)

2.3　A journey worth undertaking

A journey is made memorable by the people who live it!

As you head into defining your journey to lead this project to its rightful climax, it is worth checking that you have the lead characters identified and contributing to it.

In Chapter 1.2 we looked at where your project stands when it comes to a congruent, coherent and consistent journey. Keep those findings handy as you head into this section.

In your project, there are two things to consider when you define the remainder of its journey:

- The journey must ensure you have your leads right up to the go-live date or the farthest point they need to be on the project to be effective.

- Your journey shouldn't be enslaved to a method for the sake of it. Do not try to fit in an agile approach if it is not suitable. It is akin to asking a fish to climb a tree.

In the CONFESS section, we checked if your project journey had a clear start, stops along the way (key milestones) and a clear end. In this section, we will aim to capture any of these you identified as missing and also focus on the intersections of these, which I believe are key to a robust project journey.

Intersections and starting considerations

The key concepts we will aim to unpack are:

- passage/flow – this occurs at the intersection of the start and the key milestones

- closure – the intersection between the key milestones and the end. Without this, you will be running on spinning logs and running multiple phases at the same time with no definite closure for any of them

- focus – the intersection between the start and the end of a journey which keeps us aligned to the project outcomes and alignment to organisational strategy.

You will need to consider these concepts from abstract (visualisation) and concrete angles.

You get to make your project journey / schedule and there is no single project schedule that will fit every organisation.

What I mean here is that, as a project leader/manager, you will have to start with some initial assumptions and give them to the team as starting considerations.

This could be a go-live month (rather than specific day), or a date before which you would want to complete testing, or days when you do not want a critical set of activities to happen as you may want your organisation staff to be focused on, for example, an annual conference. This gives the leads within your team a frame of reference they can plan against.

When I started working with projects, I used to get frustrated when project managers asked me for a plan without these starting reference pointers and then pushed me down a path of significant rework each time I came up with a plan.

Over the years I figured out that your role as a project leader and manager is to facilitate your leads to be effective and this is one of many ways you can do so.

Take this HRIS implementation as an example. Some starting considerations could be:

- I have the annual remuneration review cycle happening between June and July. The revised salaries will be updated at the end of June, so I do not want us to plan a go-live date two weeks before or after 30 June.

- We need to go live with this project within this financial year, so the end of June is an absolute deadline for us to meet.

- We have the Christmas shutdown from 21 December to 4 January. Please do not plan massive activities that require organisational staff presence during this time.

Activity phases

The next step to take is to outline phases or blocks of activity and name them. This is not just a linguistic exercise but a key point in enabling flow on the project.

Dr. Arne Rubenstein is a medical doctor and counsellor who went to channel his entire work into adolescent development, developing programs that help our boys and girls successfully make a safe and healthy transition to adulthood through a concept called the Rites of Passage[1].

He has also written a bestselling book called The Making of Men which outlines the challenges our kids go through in their transition to adulthood where the enormity of physical changes in them coupled with the emotional and social changes can easily overwhelm the toughest ones and how this phase consumes a lot of our bright kids.

In the book Dr. Rubenstein articulates the need for a transition across phases during their journey punctuated by separation to visibly show where a phase ends and the next starts and yet being able to visualise it as an integrated journey.

Projects can be filled with uncertainty and ambiguity and the magnitude of them can sometimes overwhelm the best of us. One of the ways we can reduce the uncertainty and ambiguity is to break a project into phases with a logical flow across the project journey. I have seen this work well especially if you have to make sense to a wide audience of project stakeholders.

An example of how I break my projects to enable planning is:

- Phase I – Enable (Setting up and getting off the blocks)

- Phase II – Create (Designing and building the solution and its components)

- Phase III – Check (Testing to ensure fit for purpose)

- Phase IV – Launch (Business readiness and launch)

- Phase V – Nurture (Early life support)

Some of these phases could be delivered in an agile manner, especially Phase II, and I reckon this is best for the leads to discuss. Along with defining these phases, it is also important to talk with your leads and come up with three to five pointers ('success definitions') about how you will establish if each phase was successful and complete or not. Please note: some of these phases can run alongside each other for periods of time but the key is to establish what gives you confirmation about a phase finishing.

The article 'Make milestones matter with "decision gates" – stage gates with real teeth' is published on McKinsey.com[2] and discusses these success definitions as decision gates tied to further funding release. This is taking it to the next step of accountability and rigour. You may choose to do this if you want but at a bare minimum having success definitions against each phase will suffice.

Once you have articulated these success definitions, you should refer to the work you did in Section 2.1 of the ACT phase. In addition to outlining how this project aligns to organisational strategy, you also listed the outcomes and the outputs you need to produce in order to validate that the project has indeed delivered. Keep them handy.

For each of those outputs, request your leads team to work with their individual teams (and where required with each other) to come up with the list of roles and people required to complete each deliverable, and the effort they envisage from each of these roles. Follow this up with a request for two more things:

1   Identify the phase in which each deliverable needs to fall.

2   Align the deliverable to a success definition in that phase.

By performing these steps you have now created a visual flow for the project, albeit in individual teams within the overall project. You have also linked each deliverable to a phase and a measure within the phase that will establish completion. Finally you will also have a list of roles that need to be on the project to deliver it successfully.

Great work so far. This sounds easy but requires some discipline in doing and effort for the project leader/manager to articulate effectively. If not done well, your effort to create a consolidated plan across the project will start to fall by the wayside. Each time you try to make progress, you might find something that hasn't been completed from a previous phase, like the hand from the grave popping up. When you find this, you have to go back and complete it or make assumptions about it to progress a subsequent deliverable, resulting in chaos.

Workstream plan

The next step is to get the entire leads team together and outline how each lead's workstream flows across the phases. Stack each workstream plan horizontally as layers over each other. I personally recommend 'People and change' as the starting layer right at the top of the plan, as this is what the project is all about. The rest, while important, are irrelevant if we cannot get 'People and change' correct. For a typical HRIS or ERP project, I would expect to see the following streams:

1   People and change

    a   Change

    b   Training

    c   Communications

2   Functional streams including technical (recruitment, core HR, finance [record to report] etc.)

3   Infrastructure and integration

4   Data (migration and quality)

5   Reporting and analytics

6   Testing

7   Deployment

8   Support

Each of the above streams will have a layer of their own on the overall programme and will have deliverables that fall in each of the overarching phases.

Getting each of your leads to do this process in front of the full leads team gives an appreciation of the work each stream needs to do and starts to illustrate dependencies and linkages between streams. The purpose of these sessions is to flesh out these linkages and ensure the relevant leads understand this.

This also helps the leads to structure individual deliverables using a particular methodology. This process feeds significantly into sprint planning, product backlog refinement and structuring of the overall stream if they are proposing to follow a scrum or similar methodology. Equally it works if the project is planned to be delivered in a waterfall manner.

As you go through this process, you will find that some components don't fit or do not meet some of the initial pointers you gave the leads. This is OK. Note them down and organise separate sessions to explore other ways of fitting them. If you deem something impossible to fit even after a second exercise, it is worth considering if the initial pointer needs to be changed. It is important that you do this otherwise you will set the project up with unrealistic expectations.

The end outcome of this exercise should be three deliverables:

- Visual project plan on a page

- Phases constituting the plan and clear definitions of when they are deemed successful

- Deliverables aligning to the phases and their definitions and the effort required from various people to deliver them.

Point 3 in particular will be of great use when you get working on the money you need to successfully deliver the project from here on.

Have your team go through the plan individually to figure out any gaps or things that do not fit. Once done, publish it and make time to get your entire team across this plan. Depending on the audience you may have to zoom in or zoom out on this plan, but don't create separate versions for different audiences.

Make large posters of this plan and put them up on the wall. Make them visible and show progress visually. There is no better joy than moving the sliding scale pointer as you make progress in a tactile and visual manner.

You have a journey worth undertaking on your hands if the outcome of this project was deemed significant and a priority for your organisation.

Well done on pulling this together. Give yourself and your team a pat on the back and organise for a mini celebration like a morning tea or lunch or a quick round of drinks. It is worth celebrating this.

Recap and actions

At this stage of the ACT phase, you have a clear view of the following:

- Whether your project matters and, if it does, what it will produce

- Some of the people who care about this project, and the gaps that exist

- If there is a journey worth undertaking if points 1 and 2 are in place.

Over the next three chapters we will look at the remaining parts of our woodfired pizza project:

- The remaining people who matter

- Connections that click (and governance that works)

- Money we need

- Rules of engagement

Exciting times!

Essence of this section:

- Pull together a visual journey for your project. Along with a clear start, stops in between and an end, focus on the following concepts

  - flow

  - closure

  - focus.

To do:

1 Involve the leads and make sure they are consulting their teams.

2 Enable individual as well as team crafting of the journey. Be clear on the success definitions.

3 Challenge each other but focus on the consolidated plan.

To *not* do:

- Do not create the journey by yourself and give it to the team (it then becomes *your* plan, not theirs).

- Do not be rigid on the initial pointers to the extent of introducing unrealistic expectations.

- Do not have any deliverables hanging in isolation from the phases and their definitions of success.

One must-read

- 'Make milestones matter with "decision gates" – stage gates with real teeth' published on McKinsey.com[1] – *https://www.mckinsey.com/business-functions/operations/our-insights/make-milestones-matter-with-decision-gatesstage-gates-with-real-teeth*

2.4   People who care – Part II

The team

Be careful who you make memories with. Those things can last a lifetime – Ugo Eze

It is now time to use that to assemble the team that you need to successfully recover this project.

You'll use the outputs from Chapters 2.1 and 2.3 to help you through this.

First, find all the unique roles you outlined in Chapter 2.3 and list them in a spreadsheet. This gives you a full list of varied roles that you will need on the project, based on the outputs the team agrees need to be produced.

This list might seem overwhelming or like an unrealistic Christmas wish list. Don't worry about it yet.

Listing it will help you form a picture of what the team could look like. Refer to the example below.

Role	Name (if available)	Key activities	Internal / external	Month 1 (Percentage of time dedicated to project or full time equivalent)	Month 2 (Percentage of time dedicated to project or full time equivalent)
Business Lead – Recruitment		• Testing preparation • Testing execution	Internal	50%	80%
Business Subject Matter Expert – Payroll			Internal	20%	25%

In this list, it is worth starting to fill in the names you already know; there's nothing like seeing names being filled on a resourcing sheet. Start with the ones who are critical to the project.

All the roles on the project are important if your team has listed them (even though you may not agree with some of them or the amount of time they expect). It's the same in the example of triage in a military base, an analogy mentioned by Thought Leaders Business School founder Matt Church. Wounded soldiers come back to base writhing in pain and in need of medical assistance. As a doctor, you have limited capacity. What would you do?

Treat the critical cases first. Focus on the person who could die in the next hour, followed by the person who could die in the next day, followed by the one who could die in the next week.

Do the same when recruiting your project team members. If a business lead is missing on the project or the existing one doesn't have capacity, you will need to employ that person first before you employ the helpdesk support analyst who is needed three months down the line.

Use this approach to start filling in the names until you run out of names. This is the point where you will need to sit down with the key business owners and discuss the way forward. The options here could range from deprioritising something else that organisational staff are doing to allocate them on the project or backfill them with fixed term or temporary staff.

Now, this is another vital moment in your project recovery. Like the project manager, members of the existing project team have also probably had a draining experience thus far. It is even more painful for people who have been balancing a day job with their project role.

I once ran a series of interview-based webcasts where I specifically chose people who had been through this experience in their careers.

Some of the insights into how they managed this was amazing and the impacts it had on them were also varied. However, they all acknowledged that appropriate support at the right time was key to being able to manage both priorities. You can find these interviews on my LinkedIn profile.

Where I am going here is the offer to exit.

Much as you may desperately need a particular individual on the project, it is your responsibility and obligation to ask them if they *want* to stay on, and to give them an opportunity to gracefully exit. There is no point pushing someone who is already exhausted by a project into the abyss of a troubled project recovery journey.

It's like drinking water from the ocean as you try to swim ashore!

In your conversation with your current team members, you can discuss:

- the purpose of the project and how passionate they are about it

- the incentive or reward that they can look forward to upon completion of the project. It doesn't always have to be in a hefty monetary form but has to be something they value. It could be a sense of accomplishment or an enhancement in reputation they yearn for

- the effectiveness of the work they have done so far during the project recovery. Your existing project team will be able to see the difference in approach to form a sense of belonging and meaning from their role on the project.

- personal priorities and state of mind. Certain projects drive us and we are passionate about them, but personal circumstances define how we approach them. A troubled home life, an addiction, a personal battle they are facing, a physical injury or overwork could all be reasons why someone may not be in the right state of mind to be employed on a project.

Key here is having the conversation in a non-confrontational and non-judgemental manner. Remember, a project is all about people.

Even artificial intelligence and machine learning projects are implemented by humans (well... at least while I write this book 😊).

It is important while you have this conversation to also offer each team member all the support you could make available for them to play their role effectively. Be sure to include their reporting managers into these conversations so that priorities are aligned and communications are happening with the relevant people.

I was once working on a project where the national sales manager was supposed to be the key business point of contact on their sales and distribution process. For someone who was on the road, meeting customers day in and day out, the prospect of noting down a detailed sales and distribution process, followed by testing a software built for this, seemed like a death sentence. Especially when the software wasn't being delivered to enhance the sales process. It was to cater for the order taking process and beyond.

Equally they did not have much visibility into the order fulfilment process once they had made the sale. It wasn't something they handled, nor did they have interest in it. Thus far on the project, they were mandated to manage both and it was a struggle. When I took over the project, this was one of the first conversations we had and we quickly worked out that an hour or two of his inputs into the sales part of the process was about where his involvement on this project ended.

We decided to explore further within the organisation and soon found another person who was tasked with order fulfilment. This person not only had the knowledge about the order fulfilment process, but also had a keen interest in contributing to the project. They had heard about the project but were never approached for their input. Suddenly we had uncovered someone who was right beside us and keen! How good is that!

I would recommend you do more of this on your project. You really want people that have the capability, capacity and attitude to be on a project.

Keep going through this process, until you have pencilled in all the names you need against the roles your team outlined for the project. Ensure you have communicated with the people themselves and their managers to avoid any surprises.

At the end of this, you will have an internal or organisational project team ready and keen to get stuck in. Also consider any augmentation in capacity, these people may need to make things effective. This could range from tasks they hand over or get additional support on the project.

Partners (suppliers)

Partners/suppliers complete the picture when it comes to the people needed to get a project across the line.

Key reasons to engage partners include:

- a lack of key capability within the business to deliver the project

- capacity challenges with organisational staff to deliver certain parts of the project

- an expertise backed by experience that will help you significantly lower the risk for your project and also provide the guidance your internal team needs to get this project across the line.

Now, like your organisational staff, the partners (who are also people!) have been through quite a bit on the project thus far.

Some of them may have signed up to this project with certain assumptions that may or may not have been written down and agreed on. These assumptions would have led the way they structured the engagement with your organisation and in some cases also compelled them to offer a fixed price for a piece of work.

They now have a better understanding of what is needed to get this project to the finish line and a view of what their effort looks like.

The following exercises will help you understand your partners a bit better and start signifying your intent to them about reviving the project.

For the sake of consistency, we will use the same framework we used in the CONFESS phase and start with the environment.

Environment

A conducive environment must exist if there are going to be meaningful conversations with partners.

Imagine yourself in a bitter divorce or property battle. Lawyers from both parties are swarming around you and everything you say could be held against you! Do you think you would be able to have a rational conversation where you could rekindle the bond of love with your significant other? Unlikely.

It is a similar situation when it comes to mending supplier relationships during a troubled project.

If you have already reached the altar of the legal industry, this may be trickier and you will need to keep the lawyers engaged through the conversation. Trying to broker a rational conversation of mending paths while a legal procedure is underway can cause you more grief than relief.

However, if you haven't yet reached the legal eagles, then it would be worth giving this a shot.

Through section 2.3 and this one, you have established the level of effort and support you would need from a partner. The first thing to do is open a conversation, signifying your intent to genuinely make this work for both parties in delivering the outcome envisaged from the project.

This is easier said than done, especially if your project manager is external and comes from a competing organisation to the partners you have chosen. Irrespective of this, the best way to progress is to lay out the conflicts and challenges openly.

If this includes a perceived conflict of interest, be open about it and mention how you propose to manage it. Approaching conversations in this manner is your best possible bet to recover this relationship.

Alongside this, have an upfront agreement on the work you need them to keep doing, stop doing and possibly start doing while a recovery decision is made. Clarify how you expect them to work with the team and equally also clarify with your team about how you expect the relationship to work during this phase when you are in the midst of resetting the project. The internal team may not be able to get everything they need from the supplier and having this clarified upfront reduces a lot of pain for both parties.

Having set the expectations and environment under which you expect to operate over the next few weeks, it is now time to move to the other two components of a thriving supplier relationship.

Accountability

You should now better understand the effort required on your partner's behalf to deliver this project. You should also have access to the original effort and commercials that were agreed at the start.

It is now time to think about the accountability you expect them to assume. Do you want to continue operating in the same context they were initially purposed to (unlikely but worth checking), or do you want it to shift? If you want to shift, then are you clear on the direction you want them to shift?

Do you want your partner to step up or ramp down when it comes to their involvement on the project? Are there areas of expertise where they are better suited to be leveraged? For example, the way system integration organisations work in the technology industry is very different to how consulting organisations work. The system integrators are more focused on configuring and deploying their solution, and they do it well. However, expecting them to be the trusted advisor when it comes to critical business policy or processes may be stretching that expectation a bit too far.

This is where a great project manager is of value. They know exactly, by virtue of expertise and experience, how to leverage the best out of partners. Without this, you are judging a fish by its ability to fly.

Once you have determined the span of your partner's involvement, it is recommended to have that conversation with them to agree to this. Within that area of involvement, you can find the level of accountability you want them to take. This will also determine whether you make structural changes to the existing commercial structure or not. For example, if you had leveraged an existing partner in the role of a system integration partner and they had not lived up to the accountability outlined of that role, it is unlikely you will make concessions when it comes to commercials.

However, if you had signed up to leveraging a pre-built solution as is from the system integrator and midway through the project you find it unsuitable for the needs of your organisation, your perspective when it comes to discussing the accountability and commercials could be very different.

It is key to find that angle of shift you are expecting them to make from when they were originally engaged. If it is significant, then it is appropriate to have conversations about restructuring accountability and commercials. If the angle of shift isn't major but the partner's current position is a result of some assumptions or business calls they made, then they need to manage that.

'Loss leader' is a concept used by organisations at various points during their lifecycle. Some use it at the start of their organisation to get business, while some use it when new products and services are to be launched. This is where an organisation chooses to accept business from a limited number of clients or for a limited period at a price that may (just) or may not cover the costs they incur. The intention is for them to build references which will then translate to further business with those or other clients.

This can be very tricky business especially if the owners of the supplier organisation are building this with an intention to show an order book, enhance the market value of an organisation and sell it off. On the other hand, there are suppliers who genuinely want to do a great job but do price discounting to get an opportunity. Such players are more likely to benefit from an empathetic view when it comes to recovering troubled projects. But, make no mistake, a partner must have accountability irrespective of their approach to the project.

On your project, the key to a great supplier relationship is to determine that accountability.

Incentives and rewards

You evaluated the appropriateness of incentives and rewards in the CONFESS section to get a sense of how balanced and fair they are against the accountability you expected your suppliers to assume. You also had a look at factors that could be driving this, like price discounting.

At this stage, you have determined the future role the supplier could play, the environment you will make available for them and the accountability you expect them to assume.

It is time to determine the incentives or rewards you will offer in return.

This could be a review of the current contract to reflect the efforts more appropriately or change in the construct of the commercials to reflect the nature of the effort. It could also be a ramp down for the supplier in certain areas you do not see them assuming accountability for.

Data migration on technology-enabled transformation projects is a classic example of this. Most system integrators include a certain amount of effort in their contracts which is focused purely on loading data provided by the client in templates. The majority of them do not account for any of the preparatory work and guidance that a client may need to populate the load templates in the first place.

This is a classic case of caveat emptor and you need to watch out for more of these. They are spread across areas within a project including data migration, integration, people and change, support, deployment and testing.

The partners not assuming responsibility for some of these areas is ok and appropriate but if this is not articulated explicitly and hidden in some tiny piece of fine print in the contract it becomes very difficult for both parties. In such cases, it may be appropriate to segregate this piece of work from the supplier's role and be explicit about it.

Incentives must be:

- appropriate and balanced to the level of accountability you want them to assume. Equally they must be balanced for all parties

- transparent – there should be little to interpret and hidden. Equally it must outline the consequences for non-delivery.

Recap and actions

Essence of this section:

- Work needs to be done on getting the right team mix, including the

- project team

- partners (suppliers) for key external capability.

To do:

1 Identify personnel and validate with each person if they are keen to continue.

2 Align with the suppliers on accountability and incentive. Provide an environment where the partnership can thrive.

To *not* do:

- Do not push people who do not want to work on the project.

- Do not pursue aggressive and unfair negotiations with suppliers.

One must-read

Managing project teams in an age of complexity[1] *(https://www.pmi.org/ learning/library/managing-project-teams-age-complexity-7212)*

2.5   Connections that click

In Section 1.4, you looked at the connections between people on your project and what may need overhauling.

In this section, we will look at how can you can go about doing it.

We'll continue with the framework of 'expertise, empathy and empowerment' but seek to add ingredients at their intersections, which I believe will help create a strong structure with robust governance that smells less of bureaucracy and more of connections that click.

I believe three additional key elements determine whether the connections or accountabilities on your project click with the people who are responsible to implement them:

- **Trust** is built when you seek expertise and demonstrate empathy.

- **Ownership** results when empathy is backed by empowerment.

- Clear **boundaries** are visible when there is empowerment at the right level of expertise.

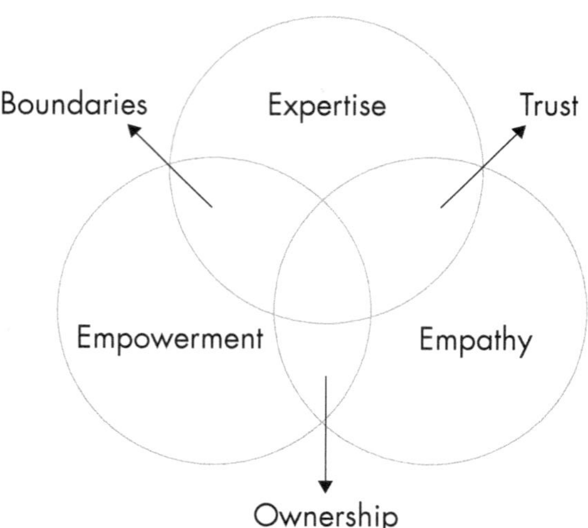

Figure 5.   Trust, ownership and boundaries.

You will use these in designing connections that click on your project.

Trust

Imagine a honey bee seeking nectar from a flower. In this analogy, the flower is the project sponsor and the honey bee is the customer/stakeholder.

The honey bee is engaged with the flower, not vice versa. It's in the honey bee's own interest to engage with the flower to seek its nectar. The honey bee trusts the flower will provide the nectar that it seeks because of the environment that exists with the flower – bright colours, visible and the peculiar fragrance.

In a project, the sponsor must create an environment where the stakeholders or customers feel comfortable that their needs will be addressed and want to start engaging. This begins when there is constant engagement between the sponsor and the customer (stakeholder) representatives.

In order to create trust between these groups, the leaders must seek expertise and demonstrate empathy.

When the COVID-19 crisis hit our world, the response from different nations was interesting. For all practical purposes, the COVID response was a 'project' that all nations undertook around the same time. Why, then, were some nations more successful in containing the impact, while others got steamrolled, losing hundreds of thousands of precious lives in the process?

Nowhere is this contrast in 'project management' more stark than the responses of New Zealand and the United States of America.

Let's start with the USA. If the president is the 'sponsor' and the American public the customers, the governors of each state could be the customer representatives. For the COVID response to be effective, the governors and the president needed be in constant communication in order to synchronise the planning and delivering of their response to the pandemic. Instead, what transpired was a sparring of words in full public view resulting in complete chaos and lost lives throughout America.

Contrast this with the New Zealand response. Right from the time it first became evident that this pandemic would not spare NZ, the government headed by Prime Minister Jacinda Ardern worked closely with the leaders in various part of the country (like council mayors and Opposition MPs) to head a coordinated response to the pandemic.

Every afternoon at 1 pm, the PM herself along with the amazing Director General of Health, Dr Ashley Bloomfield, addressed the nation, keeping the message simple, based on health expertise, and empathetic. The 'team of five million' (as she calls us Kiwis) could see that local leaders were in sync and responded appropriately to the directions.

Did mistakes happen? Sure. Did things go wrong? Sure. Did we descend into chaos? No. Because we trusted our leader, we followed her directives.

The point is that fractured relationships between the key people representing the project leadership and the customers can lead to disastrous consequences for the entire project.

Ownership

We have seen the power of empathy in structuring effective governance. We have also explored your level of empowerment within the project. At the intersection of empathy and empowerment is ownership. It is the core of why some teams and people take charge of what they are meant to do while others are dragged from meeting to meeting without progress.

Without ownership, the whole project will gather inertia and become a drag very soon. It might also be the key reason why this project got into troubled waters in the first place.

Before we delve into ownership, let us start with some exploration on connections within the project among all it's people

Formal and informal connections

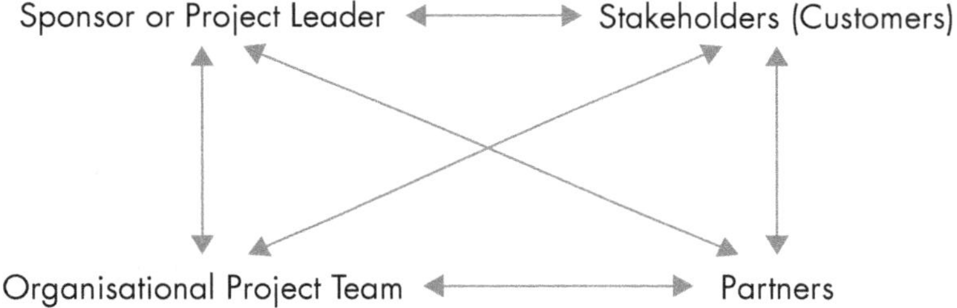

Figure 6.   Formal and informal connections

As part of project recovery it's important to focus on formal as well as informal connections between groups.

These may include the following.

Formal

- **Steering groups** are key forums that bring together the appropriate level of leaders from the stakeholders (customers) and the project leader to help provide a coordinated steer (direction) to the project.

  Representatives from the project team (normally the project manager) and partners (typically key vendor representatives) report into the steering group thus ensuring effective engagement. They do not have decision rights in the steering group but do have the remit to recommend options and way forward once they have ensured alignment with appropriate representatives.

Steering groups should comprise no more than four to six decision makers to be effective. I once walked into a project which had a steering group of close to 20 people with decision-making rights! I cannot remember a single decision that was made by that collective group. Eventually the group lost its way and became dysfunctional to the extent that we had to disband it and have a complete rejig of the entire governance.

The appropriate level of leadership is key to ensure accountability and ownership. There has been some intense discussion on the relevance of a steering group on projects following the agile methodologies. I believe a strong leadership level governance forum is indispensable irrespective of methodology.

Regularity and participation are also key ingredients to ensuring effectiveness and direction on the project.

Define the remit tightly so that everyone can put their focus into delivering the greatest value. Steering groups can get distracted and spend too much time and energy on the wrong things, which is like window shopping where you get the thrill but come home feeling exhausted and empty handed.

- **Change owners forums** help navigate teams through the change that is required to start deriving the benefits promised by the project. They are closer to ground reality when it comes to the impact of projects and hence play a critical role in the success or failure of projects.

  While a steering group can be likened to the steering controls of a car, the change owners are the engine and the fuel that will help this project reach its outcome. They are the people who will translate the leadership message to the individual teams and encourage them to participate and adopt the change. Without their engagement, it is highly unlikely that the leadership will be able to drive change required from a project.

In terms of structuring this forum or group, ensure representation from wider business units that are likely to be impacted or have an impact on the project. Ensure representation is appropriate to the magnitude of their impact or influence.

- There will be other forums you will need to enable or leverage as you progress through the recovery. Most of these are likely to exist in some form or the other within the organisation. In the interest of not making your project a 'death by groups', I would advise leveraging as many as possible that already exist in the organisation.

  For example, your organisation might have an architecture board which is responsible for ensuring that each new application or technology is aligned to the organisation strategy on technology and business architecture.

  You may already have a data governance board within your organisation. If so, feel free to leverage it. Otherwise, just get the key change owners and people responsible for ensuring data quality together at frequent intervals to track how you are progressing on data.

  Similarly make explicit structures for how you will engage and interact with suppliers beyond the routine interactions. Which forums would you like them to be represented on? How would you like to communicate with them and what are the escalation mechanisms you can leverage when needed. This applies not only for professional services suppliers but also product suppliers.

Informal

Some other connections you may want to consider include one with your partners, your project team (like a monthly morning tea) and stakeholders, which allows you to keep in touch and also build trust in addition to giving each group and people within it an avenue to reach out to other groups without having to wait for an issue to trigger that.

These connections help build the bonds you need to bring joy into your project. A place where people are excited to come to and work with like minded folks. A place that is not a drag to get through 8 hours of a working day.

Enabling these is a key aspect of project leadership.

Having had a look at the connections, here are some key ways to enable ownership:

- Be explicit with expectations and accountability. What are specific people accountable for and what does success look like in their role within the project?

- Keep autonomy and authority clean. You do not want to symbolically empower someone to make decisions while nurturing a secret desire to control their decisions.

- Be clear on the consequences. Some of these might be behavioural (and we will discuss this in the next section – 2.6) but some are related to accountability and autonomy.

For example, if you have selected a project manager and agreed on accountability when it comes to successful delivery of the project, make sure you give them control of the budget and the constraints to be aware of.

Be explicit on what budget decisions can be taken autonomously and what needs to follow a governance path. Be clear on the consequences of budget overruns and the PM's responsibility in keeping you and the steering group informed of financials.

However, do not go and play around with the cost models or make cost decisions that you just agreed would be the PM's remit. This brings us to boundaries.

Boundaries

Clear boundaries are visible when people at the right levels of expertise are empowered.

How often have you seen a steering group comprising of the head of HR, CFO, CEO and other senior level leaders in a firm (not necessarily a technology firm) discussing software products with great passion and suggesting they know more about the software than the software producers themselves?

How often have you seen critics across the project suggesting they could do a particular bit of work better than the person in charge of doing it?

How often do you find that your project manager is the best technical expert on the project but when asked for the project status, financials or risks they have no clue?

I call this being 'stuck in someone else's identity'. The final key to having connections that click on a project and governance that works is avoidance of being stuck in someone else's identity. If the right expertise is sought and secured on the project, it completes half the job. If they are empowered to then take decisions in their areas of expertise while others don't do it for them, the boundaries become clear.

This means if you are a business subject matter expert and not an architect, don't make architectural decisions. Let the right experts do it. As a business process subject matter expert, state your requirement and let the experts propose options through which you could achieve it.

Having the right boundaries will also ensure focus and the project will naturally start moving towards desired outcomes.

Recap and actions

Essence of this section:

- Connections that click and governance that works rely on expertise, empathy and empowerment.

- Combining these three will enable trust, ownership and boundaries.

- These will allow focus and engagement on the project leading to greater outcomes.

To do:

1   Ensure the formal ones have a system which includes remit, representation, cadence, what they discuss and what decisions they make.

2   Leverage existing governance forums within the organisation where it is not specific to the project.

3   Encourage more connections that click which allow people to engage with other people groups and share ideas while retaining their boundaries.

To *not* do:

- Do not make every connection a formal governance forum and pack a whole lot of people in them. We are people and not robots. We are only engaged when we see value.

- Be loose on boundaries. This is often where projects get into trouble when people overstep their remit and there is no mechanism to manage this.

- Do not do this only as a formality and go on a documentation (garbage producing) overdose.

One must-read

- McKinsey article on Digitising the delivery of government services[1] (*https://www.mckinsey.com/business-functions/mckinsey-digital/our-insights/digitizing-the-delivery-of-government-services*)

2.6   The rules of engagement

You addressed the need for guiding principles for your project in the CONFESS phase. In this section, we will look at how to go about implementing these in a manner that does not become a drag.

Guiding principles are key to steering projects to success. If a shared purpose is the glue that binds people together on the project, I reckon guiding principles are like the concrete mixing transport trucks that keep them moving.

Within the drum of the concrete mixer, the contents remain in an agitated yet controlled state, helping the concrete retain its liquid state while being pushed deeper into the drum during transport.

Well planned and articulated guiding principles cover four specific aspects: Be, Think, Do, Say.

The model below is a representation of these aspects and the elements they generate.

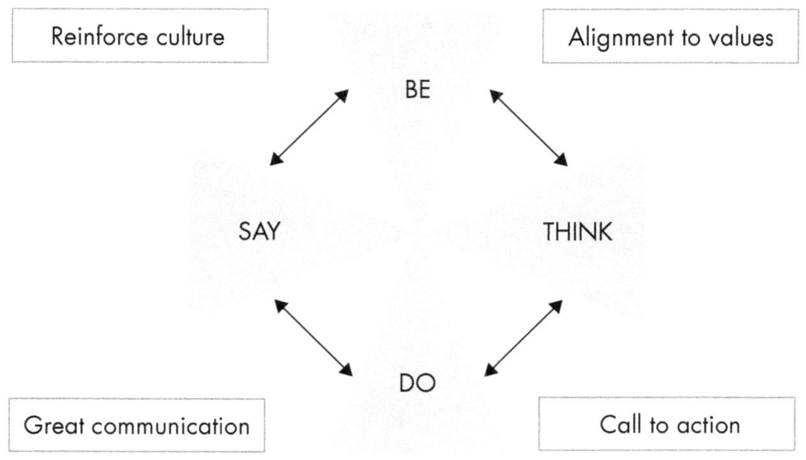

Figure 7.   Be, Think, Do, Say – Rules of engagement

Be

Guiding principles need to have a 'be' statement at the very start. This sets expectations on behaviours both as an individual and as a team. On one side, it covers expected behaviours and on the other side it lays out consequences for violation of these. Finally, this statement lays out what the project's outcomes (not outputs) will be seen as.

For example:

- 'We will *be* open, honest and proactive in our conversations.'
- 'We will *be* value add, not just additive.'

Elaborate on the principle and outline what they mean with examples. Also be clear on the consequences for deviations.

Cultural attitudes are key to the success of organisations and the projects they choose to do. I reckon that cultures are a representation of the values an organisation holds, and values are essentially beliefs that we hold dear and will very rarely change. Most of our values reflect in our *being* as individuals and teams.

Focus on the following when drafting a 'be' guiding principle:

- Outline the value or values you want this principle to embody.
- Outline expected or model behaviours as well what is not acceptable.
- Draft, review and refine the guiding principle.

Remember to keep them simple, understandable and finally actionable.

Think

Given the uncertain and evolving nature of projects, a 'think'-oriented guiding principle is another essential.

A guiding principle that shapes the thinking on a project will go a long way in not only aligning teams to outcomes but also in speeding up decision making. Every time you are confronted with a crossroad decision to make, these guiding principles will steer you towards a decision more quickly. Practised well, over time, these will get ingrained into the team's ethos and you will notice a visible and measurable difference in the pace of decision making as well as thinking.

Great software as a service implementation projects generally have a principle such as 'Adopt not adapt'. This is a simple yet extremely powerful guiding principle.

During an HRIS implementation at Auckland Council, we used this principle to great effect and in one case reduced process workflow approval steps for a number of processes from five to eight approvals down to three. Imagine the enhancement in empowerment, speed of decision making and reduction in processing time a move like this would have for an organisation that had approximately 9,000 people working. And, guess what, one of their key focus areas at that point was about enabling a high-performance workforce. How well does that sit?

Similarly when the Vodafone group implemented their flagship transformation programme, EVO[3], they had a core business model which covered fit for purpose processes for companies across the group. These was used to setup their global shared service operations across finance, supply chain and HR resulting in significant benefits across the group. Alignment to the core business model (CBM) was a key guiding principle across their implementation in different countries with very few exceptions resulting in a world class finance operations setup.

I would recommend you always have a 'think' guiding principle within your set of principles and make it short, sharp, crisp and closed to interpretation. A 'think' principle is a clear call to action.

Do

I am sure most of you have used maps on your phone to get somewhere.

A 'do' statement spurs progress as part of your guiding principles. A 'do' principle specifically directs action and helps prevent inaction. It's like pressing 'start' on Google Maps to begin receiving directions – otherwise, you might never move. Remember, projects are a venture into uncertain and uncharted territory and you do need a map.

In the CONFESS section of this book we spoke about paralysed decision making, stalled committees and painful meetings. All these issues point back to an inability to 'do' things, so it's clearly necessary to have a very clear 'do' guiding principle that shapes our actions on projects.

To begin, find a value that your organisation holds dear.

Let's look at the software company Atlassian as an example[1]. One of their values is to 'Build with heart and balance' – that is, balancing a passion and urgency with wisdom and consideration. But the final line, or what I reckon as their equivalent of the 'do' principle, stands out to me: 'Then we make the cut, and we get to work'.

This statement emphasises the need to consider aspects carefully but once that is done, it places great emphasis on the need to *do*.

When writing your 'do' principle, keep the following in mind:

- It has to spur action in unmistakable terms, meaning it cannot be open to interpretation.
- It has to link back to an organisational value.

An example of such a guiding principle:

- We will make decisions on the project, even if some are possibly incorrect. If we cannot decide, our governance forum will, else our sponsor will.

Say

A 'say' principle sets boundaries and expectations and allows people to voice their thoughts effectively. It reinforces the culture and values of the organisation and therefore of the project.

Some examples of good 'say' guiding principles that I have come across include:

- 'We say what we think but we care for how we say it.'

- 'We speak our mind but balance it with our heart.'

In the article 'How to communicate effectively in times of uncertainty' published on McKinsey.com[2], the authors prioritise communicating simply, clearly and frequently. The stress of a troubled project limits people's capacity to absorb information, and you need to communicate with them in simple terms so you don't add to the overwhelm[2].

The article also mentions that it requires nine to 21 repetitions of a message to maximise perception among an audience. If a message is not simple, clear and frequent, our brains just might not be able to process it.

The authors' other priority in communicating effectively is candour over charisma. This means the need to be honest, share and acknowledge feelings and above all give people around you a view of what shapes your decision or thinking.

Keep these priorities in mind when communicating with your team and when drafting your 'say' guiding principle.

In writing a 'say' principle, consider the following:

- It should apply to everyone across the project.

- It should outline the acceptable and the unacceptable.

Having a good 'say' statement reinforces culture and fosters a great environment where people feel safe enough to speak out, and take care in how they speak.

The key to having guiding principles that help you steer your project effectively is to first draft them, make them visible and practice them throughout the project duration.

They must underpin every behaviour and decision making on the project. Call people out if they are deviating from them without a great reason.

Be aware of the explicit reason in situations where you or your team may have to deviate from a guiding principle.

Bring them up in key meetings to see whether they are being embodied.

After you have put in all the effort to draft them, do not let them go waste by not embodying them. Don't let them become the new year resolutions, majority of which fade away before the end of January.

Recap and actions

Essence of this section:

- Given projects are a journey through uncertainty, guiding principles give a sense of direction.

- Guiding principles need to have four components:

  - 'Be' to guide alignment to values and outline acceptable and unacceptable behaviours .

- 'Think' to aid clarity of thought

- 'Do' to spur progress

- 'Say' to reinforce culture.

To do:

1   Draft guiding principles and align them to values.

2   Outline acceptable and unacceptable aspects to the guiding principles.

3   Invest in developing these with the team and get buy-in from people to commit to them. Then focus on embodying them in everything you do.

To *not* do:

- Do not fill these with jargon or make them open to interpretation.

- Do not come up with these with just a couple of individuals (or worse, by yourself).

- Do not make this a huge list which will lose relevance and interest.

One must-read

- Atlassian's Company Values on their website[1] *http://atlassian.com/company/values*

2.7   The money we need

In the CONFESS phase, we looked at two key aspects of money needed on a project:

- **Secured** – What is the budget that has been secured for the project?

- **Governed** – How is the budget governed?

You also noted down assumptions that linked directly to funding.

In the ACT phase, we will work through the money we *need* (not necessarily the money we *want*). Done right, this resets a great foundation on which the project can thrive and deliver its stated outcomes.

By this stage in the ACT phase, you should have a good idea of the following:

- Whether this project still fits with and caters to your organisational strategy and expected outcomes

- The people (and partners) you need to take you there, and how much of their time is needed.

- A view of clicking connections, robust governance and how they will be enabled

- A view of the journey ahead with the start, stops along the way, and the end

- A set of guiding principles that will steer your journey.

It is worth remembering that for any project to exist, it must answer the fundamental *'why'* in the business case.

The ultimate outcome obviously is that the business will be better off for this investment and that is worth pursuing over multiple other opportunities you could chose to execute.

If that '*why*' doesn't hold ground any longer, the logic of progressing further must be questioned.

Assuming the reason for your project to exist is still robust and defensible, let us move forward.

In my experience, a robust estimation consists of three aspects:

- Goods (including external professional services)
- Time
- Risk

Goods

This will almost always be the biggest money pool. It covers things like:

- software licenses/subscriptions, infrastructure costs (servers, cloud subscriptions)
- professional services and expertise in the following areas
    - project management
    - functional and technical expertise
    - data
    - change management
    - testing
    - deployment and support
    - technology infrastructure and integration
    - consulting or advisory expertise
    - reporting
    - coordination

- quality assurance from the product vendor, a mobile app or complementary technology, technical quality reviews, programme quality reviews and other specialised goods/services.

When estimating the cost of all these goods, use the work you did in Section 2.3. This will help you:

- plan the key blocks of work that link up to form the consolidated plan

- identify the deliverables that will be produced for each of these work packages and the requirement/effort that the goods portion will need to cater for these

- schedule the timing for when you need them.

It is important you use these as key inputs into your costing of goods in this context.

For example, software subscriptions generally come in yearly or monthly packages when it comes to software as a service offerings. Within them, you may have (and it is a good technique to try even if you haven't originally) a different mode of being charged during the project lifecycle. When you are in project mode, the number of users who use the solution is a small subset of what the eventual user base will be, and this may vary over the duration of the project. Do you have a view of how this will be charged and can you spread it across the project lifecycle? If the answer is yes, it will give you a view of how to spread it out in your project cost model which will help with the cash flow, if not the overall budget.

Similarly, with professional services, there are two scenarios – the problem of a wasted buffet or the problem of hunger!

You might sign up all the professional services and external partners from Day 1. This could be great, or it could cause your project to bleed money if you cannot utilise them effectively. It's like a buffet where you fill up your plate and then run out of room to eat it all, in the process wasting food and still paying for the entire buffet.

On the other hand is the problem of hunger or scarcity where you are watchful of every dollar you spend to the extent that you find yourself without the required expertise at the right time. This is a worse problem to have as you start falling behind on delivery and then need to overcompensate to catch up.

On your project, the work blocks, their placement on a schedule, deliverables and contribution of various goods and services to produce them should give you sufficient information to spread the costs optimally without 'overeating' or starving yourself.

Use the collective expertise of the team instead of cobbling these up by yourself in a closed room. This is often a mistake rookie project leaders and managers make, resulting in a plan that no one has contributed to or bought into, and, worse, with no validation on its accuracy and feasibility.

It's difficult to estimate accurately when it comes to costing blocks like system integration testing. One approach used by many project managers is to employ the entire professional services team on a full-time basis during that period. Another approach is to take this as a percentage of design and build efforts and estimate accordingly. Whichever way you estimate, make sure you are explicit in the assumption you are making as it will help if things shape up differently to how you planned.

Finally, consider overheads that you need to factor in. Whether your project requires your organisation to organise a separate working space or you need to factor in stationery, team rewards, lunches or any other overheads, these all cost money and are important to the overall project success.

Time

This is an area where a lot of organisations and project leaders fall into a trap. They underestimate the amount of time required of their own people to get the project delivered. Often most of these people also have a day job which is equally (or sometimes more) important and, without proper planning, these people are placed under severe stress to balance both.

This can result in angst, burnout, stress, compromised quality and, worse, overspend on goods and services.

Your work from Section 2.4 will give you a view of which people and roles within your organisation need to allocate time for the project, and at what points in time.

For example, during the design and build phase where your team members contribute to design decisions and validate the build (this works for both agile and waterfall), the workload is likely to be heavy and they might need to allocate 50% of their time to the project. Equally there might be a period when the external partners are busy developing or configuring applications and you only need to schedule time from the organisational people for ad hoc clarifications or validations.

Irrespective of what the percentages are, the key here is to produce a time profile that matches the way the project is proposed to be delivered.

This gives you three key insights:

- A profile of your organisational people's time required through the duration of the project

- A reality check on the amount of time that will be consumed (allowing for a conversation on whether people have that capacity or not). This will also inform the amount of negotiations you may have to enter if these people spread their time across multiple initiatives

- If there are specific capabilities that the project requires in terms of expertise that are not available currently.

With the first two bullets above, you will be able to plan and ensure that the efforts of the right people within your organisation are prioritised effectively.

With the third, you will get a sense of any additional capability that you may have to bring in for the project to be successful. This would also have a bearing on the overall costs. It is like bringing in a business analyst to complement and support your key business subject matter expert so that a lot of workload around articulation of requirements, validation and documentation could be taken up by someone else.

One technique I use on the projects I deliver is to ask the external partners to provide an estimate of how much time they require from the organisational staff based on their experience of delivering projects for other clients. This gives your costing more robustness and helps in estimating effectively.

Now, depending on your organisation's policies on capitalisation of staff time and internal labour rates for projects, you can incorporate this in the cost model to give a sense of money that the internal staff will consume by virtue of contributing to the project.

Some organisations take a punt here and are ambiguous about how they approach this. They do not explicitly factor in the time of organisational employees, assuming people can balance their workloads, only to realise when trouble comes knocking while leaving people stressed and miserable. If there is one thing you can do right, this is it. If the project is important and relevant for your organisation and its strategies, make the best people available to help deliver it.

Including the cost of organisational staff in your estimate is also a way of ensuring that you are prepared for eventualities where you may need to backfill some of your organisational staff with temporary or contract staff to help them devote time to the project.

One final thing to consider, and this depends on how deep you want to go while planning the budgets, is how much tolerance you have for variations. During various stages of the project you will inevitably involve people beyond the set of individuals you are forecasting for. This could be for things like user acceptance testing, developing champions or ambassadors within business units to facilitate the change management, or providing support for queries after the project goes live.

Most organisations approach this with a view of planning in advance and just making people available for these but I have also seen organisations including those in the project costs. I prefer the former as the relative effort is low compared to the process of explicitly budgeting them in.

Risk

Risk is a possible deviation to the way things are planned, resulting in consequences that need to be faced.

Any project, irrespective of the methodology or framework it adopts, faces risks. Some of them can be foreseen and managed while some are unforeseen. Every project needs to have a risk management approach which includes proactive identification and management of risks.

These should feed every component of the project including the end destination, journey, people, connections/governance and guiding principles. It is like driving a car on the motorway – you need to keep an eye on vehicles around you, the road ahead, your fuel level and state of your car, and your energy levels.

There are numerous approaches organisations take to account for risk on a project. Some are as simple as allocating an additional percentage of the cost of goods and time. Depending on how accurate your estimations of goods and time are, this may not be a bad approach. However, it comes with pitfalls because you haven't fully understood the risk profile that exists on your project and while this may not impact you too much from a budget perspective, it is likely to cause other issues when it comes to delivery.

When it comes to risk, the Project Management Body of Knowledge (PMBoK)[1] and other frameworks prescribe various techniques to quantify risk on a project. Important among all of these is to run a risk identification exercise with key stakeholders and get a diverse view on the profile. Each stakeholder, including people within your project, can contribute rich detail in their areas of operation when it comes to risk.

Once identified at a management level, you need to review the risks that need addressing and how you would like to address them. Not all risks need mitigation. Some are even accepted. The key is being aware of them. A great project manager thrives in risk and this is where they deliver value.

For the risks you have identified as needing mitigation, you may want to go further into some detail and allocate money based on the consequences of the risk materialising or use some formulae that is accepted within your organisation to quantify the money that needs to be allocated for risks.

Typically, depending on the size of the project and the cost for goods and time, it is good to allocate a percentage or set amount for change requests. This is separate to the money you need to manage the risks identified on the project. Obviously this money has to be governed and needs to go through an approval process before it is sanctioned for use, but it ensures that you are not scrambling when it comes to funds on a project.

You will note that I haven't mentioned anything specific about unknown risks. These are risks that are difficult to envisage within the context of a project but exist in the context of the organisation and the environment it operates in. For example, your company could be taken over by another company during the project. Or a new regulation in response to some event may suddenly cause your project to accommodate significant changes. These are quite difficult to quantify and while you could have a list that points to them, estimating for the impact of these can be a difficult ask with little value. Most organisations have a specific percentage set at an organisation level to deal with these. I would go with this approach to keep it simple.

Assumptions

Before we close this chapter we need to consider assumptions.

Assumptions are a powerful tool when it comes to projects. Given the uncertainty that surrounds technology-enabled transformation projects, assumptions provide direction to navigate the uncertainty. They call out key pillars and foundation blocks you are using to build the project on. They also give you context when you review the project down the line on why things happened the way they did and what directed certain responses to certain situations.

They are like waypoints on an aircraft flight path. They provide you a sense of direction and navigation throughout the flight.

It is important to list the assumptions you have made while devising the recovery story on your project. In addition, it is a good exercise to list what will happen if any assumption is invalidated. Similar to each risk having a consequence when materialised, assumptions have impacts when invalidated and having a view of this helps the leadership and management picture the consequences – if there are any that they don't feel comfortable fronting up to, they could change the assumption now.

I was once involved in a packaged software application implementation where there was an assumption that we would be able to leverage a standard connector provided by the application to consume data from it. This meant our integrations to some other systems had to be architected in a certain manner to make this work. Mid way through the discovery phase we realised that the standard connector needed additional work to be useful to us and this meant we needed more time and hence potentially more cost. However, we had built in a check point during the planning to determine whether our assumption was correct and had outlined what it would mean. This helped us navigate the not so good news in a planned manner.

The key to effective money management on any project is having clear definitions of success at each decision / stage gate and continually validating / invalidating assumptions proactively.

Recap and actions

Essence of this section:

- Use the work you have done on the destination, journey, people and connections to estimate for goods, time and risk.

- Devote time to assumptions and what happens when they are invalidated.

- For any areas where it involves complexity (like data, change) validate that experts in those areas have had inputs into the estimation and that they have engaged the appropriate organisational staff to come up with this.

To do:

1 Use the goods, time and risk view to estimation.

2 Articulate assumptions and consequences.

3 Understand your organisation's policies on unknown risks and
accommodate these within your budget.

To *not* do:

- Do not build buffer on buffer (flab) to provide safety nets.

- Do not try and drill down to extreme details at the cost of time.
If experts contribute to the estimates, you will see the value of
experience adding robustness to your budget.

- Do not make judgement calls and cut funds in areas that you
feel bullish / heroic about.

One must-read

- The article 'The science of uncertainty: Blown budgets
and destroyed schedules? Sometimes, it's weak project
estimation that's to blame' published by Project Management
Institute[2] (*https://www.pmi.org/learning/library/
science-uncertainty-project-estimation-11520*)

3

RESOLVE

3.1   The destination

In the CONFESS section of this book, you looked at the destination this project could lead you to and the missing pieces in getting clarity. Following that in the ACT stage, you worked through the missing pieces.

Here we are at the RESOLVE stage where you will make the decision (if you haven't already) to recover this project or kill it elegantly.

Matt Church, the founder of Thought Leaders Business School[1] and author of multiple books, links the word 'decide' to other words in that family like homicide and suicide, which essentially mean 'to eliminate'. Matt refers to the process of decision making as a qualified process of elimination of options.

As we get into this critical phase, it is important to acknowledge that the decision you will make for this project will be the right one. I say this because there is a stigma attached to closing projects, and I find that amusing.

As the project leader, it is always important to be aware of what difference a project makes to the overall chosen journey of an organisation. If we hang on to projects just because we are entrenched in them, it quickly turns into an addiction which can lead to disastrous consequences.

Let us delve a bit into a decision-making framework that will help us objectively assess whether to recover a troubled project or not.

There are three parameters to consider:

- **On the journey** – Is a project producing a product that takes you further on the journey your organisation wishes to follow?

- **Bridging a gap** – Does the product bridge a gap or lay a beam to complete the bridge on the journey?

- **Valued by people** – Will people use the product or service produced by this project to take them further on the organisational journey?

I use the analogy of a 'bridge to nowhere' during this part of a troubled project recovery, using the example of a new bridge over the river Choluteca in Honduras[2]. Honduras is a Central American country prone to severe hurricanes; any structure built there needs to be strong enough to stand up to nature's fury. The bridge was built in just over two years and was hailed as a construction marvel.

A few months after the bridge was built, Hurricane Mitch struck Honduras. The hurricane caused massive damage to lives and property across Honduras. While the bridge itself survived, the hurricane caused the river to change course. Instead of the river flowing beneath the bridge, it now flows besides it. Overnight the bridge became useless and is famously known as the 'bridge to nowhere'.

Now, while organisations do not usually change their direction or strategy overnight, there are ample examples of such decisions being taken in a relatively short space of time. The COVID pandemic is a classic example of such a situation where organisations were forced into quickly reviewing and prioritising projects.

Your project must be scrutinised to evaluate if it is still relevant to your organisation's mission and strategy.

Whether the project creates a foundation for the journey, or delivers a critical piece on the journey itself, it must be relevant to the journey.

If it's not, your project is likely to be a bridge to nowhere.

On the journey

A word of caution while evaluating your project on this parameter: it is important to understand what your organisational journey (mission and a chosen set of strategies) is and how your project links to it.

Take the example of the Sydney Opera House[3]. Viewed narrowly, the project could be deemed a failure with massive overruns on budget and time in construction. However, it is worth noting that the Opera House hosts around 2,000 events every year with hundreds of thousands of people visiting it annually. It is the cornerstone of positioning Sydney as a vibrant metropolis. Without condoning the project management issues that plagued its original construction, the point to note here is that the Opera House was an important part of the city of Sydney's journey to position itself as a preferred destination and, on that journey, it certainly delivered. Do check which journey your project aligns to.

Bridging a gap

As well as the journey your project aligns to, it is important to check if the project produces a product or service that furthers you on the journey. All projects must produce a product or service at the end. A relevant project produces something that bridges a gap or furthers our progress on the journey. A human capital management system implementation typically reduces a lot of manual, time-consuming and draining overheads so that your employees can focus more on doing the work they were hired for.

Valued by people

The third pillar of evaluating a decision on recovering or terminating a troubled project is how much people value it. The Millennium

Dome[6] project in the UK is an example of this. Built with significant hype around it and also delivered on time and budget but was ultimately closed down on 31 Dec 2000 as it failed to attract the number of visitors forecasted. It was sold and converted to a sports arena.

In hindsight, an idea that you build such a costly monument to celebrate one occasion (dawn of the new millennium) with no foreseeable utility beyond that seems a poor one, but there were enough people at the right levels to back this at that time. However very few were the actual stakeholders who would value this post completion.

With your project, after you establish alignment to organisational strategy and a link to furthering the organisational journey, it is key to establish if there are people that value it and will support execution of the project. Finally those people will use the product / service after it is launched.

Patrick Lencioni, the author of Five dysfunctions of a team[5] and many other books, once ran a podcast on designing the world's worst job. He referred to anonymity (no one cares), irrelevance (doesn't make a difference) and immeasurement (inability to measure the difference they make) as key factors to design such a terrible job.

I have my spin on this when it comes to projects. If you wanted to structure and lead the world's worst project, then create one that has no relevance to the organisational journey, does not produce anything that is worthwhile and finally no one seems to care about it!

Having gone through this section, it should be evident to you whether your project should continue or not.

Recap and actions

Essence of this section:

- On the journey – Is your project aligned to the journey your organisation has chosen (alignment to strategy)?

- Bridging a gap – Does it produce something that provides a foundation or furthers your organisation's quest to reach a destination using the chosen road?

- Valued by people – Does it have a set of people who value it?

To do:

1　Utilise information gathered from the CONFESS and ACT stages to drive decision making.

2　Engage your project manager and key business owners in the decision making.

3　Be fact based and objective to the best extent possible.

To *not* do:

- Do not make up connections to a journey (like the pieces of a puzzle – if it doesn't fit easily it probably doesn't fit).

- Do not add or remove scope without proper assessment as it may cause problems further down the line.

- Do not try to force the project onto people's agendas just because you are invested in continuing it.

One must-read

Case study: The Millennium Dome in 'Project failure case studies and suggestion', published in the *International Journal of Computer Applications*[6], available at *https://www.researchgate.net/publication/262952882_Project_Failure_Case_Studies_and_Suggestion*

3.2   The people

*"If you take out the team in teamwork, it's just work.
Now who wants that?"*

—MATTHEW WOODRING STOVER

You're getting so close. You are on the better side of so much good work that has been done over the past few weeks on your project. You have gone from being frustrated, annoyed and disappointed to understanding what ails your project and taking steps to get it back on track.

You have visited all the key aspects of a troubled project and worked through a specific set of remedial actions that will help pulling it back on track or aid in making a logical and elegant close.

This chapter focuses on the foundation on great projects – people. You have delved deep into the people you need on the project and how to assemble them. You have also accorded attention to creating an environment where people can thrive.

Now, you are at the cusp of going through the second lever of decision making when it comes to a troubled project recovery.

From a people perspective, there are three key factors to consider in the RESOLVE phase:

- **Identified** – Have you identified all the relevant people and roles that need to be staffed for the project to deliver to its outcomes?

- **Secured** – Have you managed to secure the people you need and have a viable plan to secure the roles you don't need immediately?

- **Augmented** – Have you supplemented your internal team with the capability/capacity they are likely to require on this project?

Pretty much like a pre-take off airline check list which includes a check on all the passengers (at least the ones who make it on time 😊), the pilot and other crew members. You wouldn't fly without them.

On your project, it is key to look objectively at all the work done so far and evaluate the situation for the four main people groups (leaders, internal project team, stakeholders, suppliers) against these parameters.

Consider the following:

- Are there roles that are currently vacant that seem like a complete nightmare to resource?

- Are the business people allocated and secured for the project throughout its duration? Do they have adequate capacity to support the project or are they expected to pick this up as an extracurricular activity?

- Have you asked for help from the relevant people and got their buy-in to collaborate on the project?

- Do you have a clear view of what work you expect people to perform and how much time it is likely to take?

- Do the suppliers/partners have all the people you need and are they included in the agreements you have with them?

- Have you factored for backfills that your internal organisational team may need for additional capability?

- Finally, are there critical roles that are empty and for which a viable option for resourcing hasn't been worked out? (A project I once ran had no one to play the role of a solution architect and this was critical to get the solution structured properly.) Would you board a flight without a qualified and experienced pilot in the cockpit?

In a country like India where cricket is a religion, finding a spot in the playing 11 in a local village team is a big deal. The situation here in NZ is completely the opposite. On most Saturdays during summer you will see one guy (captain) in the cricket team scrambling to assemble 11 bodies that can move. Some hilarious moments arise when the fill-ins arrive on a cricket field and look like fish out of water. The point here is you need the right people to get the job done, not just an excuse for a team that you cobble together out of necessity.

From a decision-making perspective, if the answers to some of the above questions are not clear, it is worth pausing and evaluating whether this project can continue and, if yes, how long have you got before the project becomes bottlenecked?

Look at your project and make this resolution. You've now got the second lever of the RESOLVE phase and you are closer to making that crucial decision.

Recap and actions

Essence of this section:

- The people you need on the project should be

    - identified

    - secured

    - augmented.

To do:

1 Utilise information gathered from the CONFESS and ACT stage to drive decision making.

2 Identify gaps in the people structure and assess if you have viable plans to address them.

3 Check if there is buy-in from the relevant leaders and partners to allocating the people the project needs.

To *not* do:

- Do not assume that Peter can do the role of Paul. Some roles are specialised and without the relevant capability, you are doing the project a disservice.

- Do not try to cut people's time to make it palatable. Irrespective of automation, machine learning and artificial intelligence, it takes capable humans with capacity to deliver projects.

- Do not settle for sub-par resourcing on the project. You reap what you sow.

One must-read

- The article 'The human factor in project management' published by Project Management Institute[1] *https://www.pmi. org/learning/library/human-factor-project-management-9276*

3.3   The money

You have arrived at the final pillar of RESOLVE: the one that will help you complete your assessment on whether to progress this project into its recovery or elegantly kill it.

Money on a project is like the fuel in your car. You can have the flashiest of cars, amazing chauffeur services, great amenities and generous boot space, but it ain't moving a bit without any fuel.

You don't need all the fuel all at once to get you to our destination, but you need a plan to re-fuel where relevant to help you keep going.

In the ACT phase you worked through the budget you need to get this project to its intended outcome by creating a detailed estimate.

Now it is time for decision making.

Most organisations, irrespective of size, would have a forum or board that oversees funding requests for projects. You have now got to a position where you can take this to them and seek approval to progress.

Consider the following first.

- At the cost of sounding repetitive, consider if the original reasons behind investment in the project, as outlined in the business case are still valid. Assuming they still are, consider the next point.

- Have a clear story on what you originally set out to achieve, what you have achieved, what you have learnt and where are you proposing to go next. Be clear on the money the project needs.

- Call out the key dependencies, risks and assumptions that will help the forum make informed choices on funding.

Great job on reaching this stage.

Now, let's get to the decision making. There are three things to consider here when it comes to the budget for a troubled project recovery:

- **Covered** – Will the money you are asking for cover the spending you have to undertake (on goods, services, people's time, overheads and risks you anticipate)?

- **Supported** – Is it supported by a relevant executive who takes responsibility for successful outcomes or the failure of the project? The executive needs to believe in the project and its outcome.

- **Agreed** – Finally, there is nothing like a signed cheque. If you have done all the work in re-constituting a clear way ahead, with people that matter producing an outcome that someone cares about, with an estimate of the appropriate amount of money you need, then it has to be agreed upon at the right levels of authority for you to progress.

Assuming you have a *yes* against all three factors above, the money is good to go.

Recap and actions

- Essence of this section: money required for your project:
- covers the needs of your project
- is supported by the appropriate executives
- has been agreed on and approved by the appropriate forums.

To do:

1 Get clear on the money position.

2 If there are phased draw downs, be aware of them and the risk involved.

3 Combine the results from the Destination (Section 3.1) and People (Section 3.2) sections to make a collective decision on the go-forward option.

To *not* do:

- Do not change the approach or funding drastically at this stage in the rush to get approvals.

- Do not be tempted to push the project through even if the factors and their logical direction point against it.

- Do not commit to delivering the same outcomes for a significantly lower amount of money.

One must-read

- LEVI Strauss's SAP implementation and budget overruns.[1] (*https://www.zdnet.com/article/levi-strauss-sap-rollout-substantially-hurt-quarter/*)

3.4   All together now

Let us now look at a consolidated view of all three factors that will help you decide your go-forward position:

- **Destination** – If a project is aligned to a strategy the organisation is pursuing, and is high enough priority, then the project must progress and you should continue your recovery. If this is not the case, you could either delay or completely stop the project.

- **People** – If the destination factor gives you a go-forward approach, then you need to consider any critical gaps in your people plan and what avenues you have to address them. It is important to view this from a risk-mitigation perspective. This may mean you could delay a few activities or schedule them differently or modify your approach slightly.

- **Money** – Finally, do you have the money you need? You don't need all of it at the same time but you need approval for it. Without the money, outcomes may not be realistic and you could embark on a discussion for a different, or toned-down set of outcomes. Committing to the exact outcomes without the money you need is never recommended.

Well done on reaching this far. Based on this, you can make one of the following three high-level decisions at the end of the RESOLVE phase:

- Stop the project.

- Pause the project for a defined period.

- Continue recovering the project.

Any of these decisions will be the correct one, as you have completed the right amount of supporting work with involvement from enough other people to validate it. Never try and measure this against other organisations or other projects as they do not have the same circumstances as you.

Once you have made the decision, ensure there is collective buy-in at the governance level. You could build this as you go culminating in the final approval by the investment forum.

This should you put you in good stead for the EXECUTE phase.

4

EXECUTE

4.1   Execute

> *"Someone once asked Somerset Maugham if he wrote on a schedule or only when struck by inspiration. "I write only when inspiration strikes", he replied. Fortunately, it strikes every morning at 9'o clock sharp.""*
>
> — STEVEN PRESSFIELD IN THE WAR OF ART.[1]

Welcome to the EXECUTE stage of your project. By this stage you have gone through the toughest parts of the recovery journey and have come out stronger irrespective of the decision you have made on the direction your project will take.

At this stage, you will have made one of three decisions:

- Close the project.

- Pause the project for a defined period of time.

- Continue the project with a refreshed setup.

In this chapter we will go through an approach that will act as a compass to guide your way back.

There are four areas to look at (three key ones and a fourth which is influenced by the others).

- People and purpose

- Rules and connections

- Deliverables and dates

- Money

Our approach to these will be based on the outcomes we expect to see, that will eventually get us to a logical closure of our project.

Treat it like a flight that has taken off against strong headwind and now is at cruising altitude. The odd turbulence will come in its way, so will the odd lightning strike. Yet the flight continues to navigate and cruise through these, flying across time zones with the sun making appearances and vanishing as you speed towards your destination.

The crew go about their roles serving you and the pilot interacts every now and then till we reach a point ready to descend for landing.

There will be a flurry of activity, both from the crew and the passengers to get themselves ready for the landing. The pilots in the cockpit are constantly communicating with the crew and the passengers even while they are diligently going through a checklist for landing and communicating with the air traffic control on ground.

And then, the moment arrives where you feel the rubber hit the road (literally), followed by a sudden bout of speed, finally coming to rest, ready for you to disembark, complete airport formalities and head to your intended destination.

Our project from now on, is like the flight. Depending on the decision that was made regarding the project in the RESOLVE phase, we will look at each of the 4 areas and our approach to ensure a smooth landing.

Before we dive into this, refer to the model below to help you frame this up in your mind and navigate the remainder of the project journey:

Area	Approach	Result
People and purpose	Obsess about	Buy in
Connections and rules of engagement	Insist on	Alignment
Deliverables and dates	Place value	Outcomes
Money	Watch	Control

Figure 8. Execute – Focus areas

Irrespective of the decision that was made, all four components of the model are still relevant, though their nature and magnitude may vary.

Option 1 – Close the project

People and purpose

There are people on your project who have been part of this journey with you and this decision will impact them in various ways. Focusing on them as you wind the project down is probably the best thing you can do.

For organisational staff, facilitate options where they could pursue another project that may benefit from their services or offer them the option to settle back into their operations role.

If they choose to pursue options beyond your organisation, support them with recommendations or being their referee. Write them a recommendation that recognises the contribution they made to the project while it was running.

A bit of extra attention is required for people who were seconded to the project and backfilled or replaced with someone else so that they could help accord focus to the project. Now you have a problem of two people with one role and it is neither's fault.

For external people like consultants and contractors, the same points could be applied except for allowing them to settle back into operational roles.

Ensure a proper closing down event (it could be as simple as a shared morning tea) to acknowledge people's contributions and wish them all the best.

Rules and connections

When closing down a project, ensure that all the governance forums are communicated with and everyone has a clear view of the closing-down plan and timelines.

The way you choose to communicate is dependent on the timing and circumstances prevailing within the organisation at the time. Earlier in 2020 I was involved in closing a project one month after we had mobilised an entire team and governance groups. This decision was in response to the emerging COVID situation. Clearly it was not possible to convene all the governance groups and inform them personally. The executive leadership within the organisation decided to pick this up and communicated to each of the governance forums and key organisational staff involved. The result was a closer bonding that became established among those involved. This included the external partners, to whom they expressed their acknowledgement and ensured a fair and proper exit.

Deliverables and dates

Even as part of the closing-down process, there are deliverables and dates to be met. Placing value of these is imperative to a proper close.

It's like a flight cancellation in response to a severe weather event. The people responsible for the flight, right from the pilots to cabin crew and airline staff on the ground, have things to complete before a flight can be considered cancelled.

On a project there will be things that need to get done. Here are some things to consider:

- Storing of relevant documentation generated during the project. Some of these could be useful in your day-to-day operations even without the project progressing. Watch out for them. Gold dust!

- Organising for return of equipment and property that would have been given to project people.

- Closing commercial agreements and contracts.

- Checking other compliance-related deliverables like communications and checklists that may be required by external agencies.

Money

All the above factors have a money component and need careful monitoring as you progress through project closure.

Consider:

- obligations arising from financial contracts and payments to be made.

- any ongoing payment agreements and negotiations that need to happen.

- notice period pays for external partners including contractors.

- any penalties or early termination fees that need to be considered.

Making a list of all these considerations on your project will ensure your project doesn't continue to bleed the organisation after it is closed down.

Option 2 – Pause the project for a defined period of time

Generally, this option is chosen when the project team, the leadership and the stakeholders decide that they cannot take this project on at this time, but it remains important to the organisation and its strategy.

A defined stand-down period is outlined with the intention that the project will be picked up on the other side of that period.

All of the four aspects touched upon in Option 1 are very much relevant here with the addition of needing to outline considerations for resumption. The key differences are noted below.

People and purpose

Unlike closing the project down, this option has a purpose element to it. As such, it is important to re-emphasise the purpose and relevance of this project.

You should:

- communicate with key stakeholder groups on the purpose of the project and how it will resume

- outline an approach on how the needs this project would have met will be addressed in the interim (it could be a relaxation in expectations or additional staff to support)

- outline when the project is likely to be revived and who you would love to have on it.

When it comes to people on the project, do all the things outlined in Option 1. You will also need to have conversations with key people groups on expectations of a return.

Now the biggest challenge here is that while there is intent to revive the project after a defined period of time, it is subject to an environment that is rapidly changing.

The leadership within the organisation may change, the market dynamics may change, key people could leave the organisation, the organisation could be sold, or the solutions underpinning the project could change. The possibilities are endless.

I was once involved in a project to implement SAP enterprise resource planning (ERP) for an organisation that was taken over by another organisation. Essentially the project had been put on ice for a defined period of time for various reasons and was now being revived.

The original owners of the company had plans to implement S/4 HANA, the latest version of SAP's ERP solution, but now had to settle in for SAP ERP (ECC), the older version of the same software. This required a slightly different set of people capabilities to implement. Also considering it was an older version, the new owners wanted to invest far less than the previous ones because there was acknowledgement that they would have to upgrade in a few years after the implementation. Around this time, the leadership within the company had changed significantly with various key positions being vacant.

As you can see from the above example, reviving a project with all these changed factors is a significantly different and potentially more challenging task.

The key here when it comes to people and purpose is to articulate the intent to revive, yet be realistic about things that could influence your plans. This helps people from clinging on to false hopes and be more forward looking in what they would like to do with their careers.

When it comes to partners/suppliers, while it is tempting to try and hold on to capability through retainer agreements or the like, the fact remains that this costs money and you may not have the money. Equally, your partner capability may be suited for a fast-paced and dynamic environment. Putting them on retainers may suck the energy out of them and you are likely to see entire dynamics change.

Putting a project on hold can be more difficult than closing it down or deciding to continue on a recovery path. Be as it may, it is a tightrope to balance when it comes to winding down and setting expectations around revival without locking the organisation into liabilities.

Rules and connections

While most of the activities are similar to Option 1, consider what forums or connections you would like to keep going even when the project is not running.

For example, you may have set up a forum which includes people across the business to review data cleansing and data quality enrichment. Now even when the project is not in play, this is something you may want to continue under normal operations. The systems put in place by the project may well continue to be utilised by the organisation.

However, the remaining formal setups like the steering group or tribe may be worth ramping down completely as they cease to be relevant.

Deliverables and dates

All the points mentioned in Option 1 apply here as well with the following additions:

- Do you want to articulate a plan to ramp up the project after the hiatus? If yes, how detailed would you like it to be?

- Do you want to articulate a plan for parts of the project that could be incorporated into the business to ensure some form of continuity during the stand-down period?

Money

Consider all the points mentioned in Option 1. In addition to this, there are a few pointers worth considering when putting the project on hold:

- Review the commercials with contractors to explore if any of their existing services or people could be re-deployed to another project or operational part of the business. Be sure to involve your legal team in this as statements of work and contracts are specifically drawn out for individual projects. If these were purely time and materials type contracts, then it may be easier to explore alternative options. In most other cases, it may be more feasible to terminate contracts by mutual agreement and close them off.

- In some cases, suppliers may be willing to have a delay incorporated in the contract for a brief period without alteration to terms and conditions. See if this is relevant to your project.

Option 3 – Continue the project with a refreshed setup

Now we are talking!

You have gained great insight into what this project means to your organisation. You have:

- affirmed that project objectives still make sense and are important to organisational strategy.

- identified people who care about what the project will deliver. Equally, you have the appropriate people onboard to deliver the project successfully.

- established a clear journey with stops that are visible and you understand what each stop means.

- established the connections that click and a governance that works.

- identified clear rules of engagement that will guide your thoughts, actions, communication and behaviour on the project.

- estimated the money you need to get this delivered, and you have had it approved by the appropriate authority within the organisation.

So, what are the key things you need to do to get your project across the line?

People and purpose

Be clear on the purpose of your project. Every flight has a set destination and so should your project. However, flights must be able to adapt to turbulence, lightning strikes and other planes in the sky. Similarly, your project must also be nimble enough to keep itself aligned to the purpose which in turn is aligned to organisational strategy, which is subject to change.

You must obsess about people. The best projects are the ones that people look forward to being involved in. Engaged team members turn up with ideas, collaborate with passion and celebrate with the heart. They challenge each other, make themselves heard and understand that not all their views or approaches can be accommodated. They are fine with that – it doesn't stop them from contributing. They loathe bragging and nasty conduct. They stand up to behaviour that does not align with the environment and expectations you have set for the project.

I was involved in a project recovery in which the supplier was still not completely on board. They paid lip service to the direction the project was heading in and their contribution to it, but did not back up their words with actions. We chose to call it out in a respectful manner and asked for accountability.

Nasty responses followed, but something great happened. The rest of my team made it very clear that they would not tolerate this. They were invested in the project and its purpose and, having gone through trouble once, they were not willing to fall for it again.

They were battle scarred but wiser. Within another three months, we had replaced the supplier, changed the entire risk profile of supplier delivery, and got the project across the line.

I can't overestimate the importance of looking after the people on your project. Plan the celebrations, acknowledge the frustrations, appreciate the contributions, and have the conversations. Ask for and offer help. Support each other through the tough days and don't miss a chance to laugh together. Build relationships. They will outlive the project and you will be amazed by their magic.

When I was working in South Africa, we were ready to go live with a project. On the day, my team decided to fly out from Johannesburg to beautiful Cape Town for a short yet deserved holiday. We got off the flight at Cape Town and my colleague Karishma wanted to check a file before we could shut down and enjoy our vacation.

Disaster!

A VLOOKUP error in data had caused incorrect mapping to suppliers and resulted in a large number of purchase orders being entered against the wrong suppliers. For anyone who has done ERP implementations, the purchase order is a dreaded data set. With linkages to multiple other data sets like suppliers and products, it is a nightmare to get wrong. And yet, despite all our care and checks, we had still made a mistake!

I was in despair, but Karishma came up to me with a smile and we got to work. We found our way to the Cape Town office, spoke to the right people, thought through the problem, discussed the solution with other project members and, by evening, we had a solution.

The execution would take days, but we had isolated the problem and disarmed the rogue purchase orders. This was enough for us to go live and to enjoy our short break in Cape Town. That April day in 2013 is still fresh in my mind, remembering that it was my team that helped me sail through. That is the power of people on your project.

Rules and connections

Governance forums must be engaged and formal. Drive to an agenda irrespective of agile or waterfall. Be clear on risks, progress and messaging.

Consistency and regularity can help anyone ace it.

Don't be tempted to make that one casual exception, even when your workload is intense.

The guiding principles on the project, especially those to do with behaviour and communication, should be passionately followed with deviations called out. A brilliant jerk must not be tolerated.

I remember a programme manager once making the tough decision to let go of two or three such people because they had strayed away from the guiding principles. At the time I wondered what would become of the programme without them, but, as it later transpired, the programme would have been worse off with them and their behaviour. Finding replacements, though painful, was actually the better and easier thing to do.

Deliverables and dates

Place value on these. It is not acceptable to miss deliverables and dates just because you can. It lets you down, lets the project team down and ultimately lets the organisation down. Of course unexpected things happen on projects which need to be accommodated, but convenience shouldn't be the driving reason for this.

Any work without a deadline is best endeavours with no accountability.

Don't let deliverables on your projects be the source of your frustration. Place value on them and communicate this to the team. After all, the team has come up with the deliverables and the plan. Back yourselves to meet timelines and make the deliverables happen.

Money

Finally, watch the money! Be good with it and it will be good to you.

Great project leaders watch the money and what they are getting for it. Be across your finances and all components of it, whether it is invoicing or payments or accruals, capex or opex. Be in tune with the flow of money in and out. There is no substitute to this. If you do the people, purpose, rules, connections, deliverables and dates well on the project, the money takes care of itself but still needs watching.

Don't worry about sophisticated models and complex formulae. Keep it simple. For each bucket or category of funds, you need to know what is planned, what is spent and what the remaining forecast looks like.

Control these and you will never run a troubled project again.

What next?

If you have found yourself in the midst of a troubled project, I recommend following the approach defined in this book that starts with acknowledging trouble at the earliest possible instance.

If you are the sponsor or leader of this troubled project, I recommend you find a great project manager who can be your co-pilot on the recovery mission (if you don't already have one). Along with your project manager, core project team and your partners (suppliers), work through the CARE framework outlined in this book, trusting the process and being open and honest about it.

You can find a host of free resources on my website ganapathyiyer. com. on a variety of project related topics including how to choose a project manager, making decisions, and managing emotions while working on projects.

I work with organisations to help them embed effective project delivery within their teams through mentoring, training, facilitation and coaching.

I also write regularly on the world of projects and speak at events.

My vision is to empower and enable people within your organisation run great projects and I would love to speak with you if your organisation sees projects as a place to help people grow and in turn deliver significant growth to your organisation.

My contact details are:
Phone – +64 22 170 7827 | Website – ganapathyiyer.com
Email – *gi@ganapathyiyer.com*
LinkedIn – *https://www.linkedin.com/in/ganapathyiyernz/*

I wish you all the best and look forward to hopefully meeting and talking to you on one of your project journeys.

References

Why this and why now

1   Delivering large scale IT projects on time, on budget, and on value *https:// www.mckinsey.com/~/media/McKinsey/dotcom/client_service/BTO/ PDF/MOBT_27_Delivering_large-scale_IT_projects_on_time_budget_ and_value.ashx#:~:text=Takeaways-,On%20average%2C%20large%20 IT%20projects%20run%2045%20percent%20over%20budget,very%20 existence%20of%20a%20company.*

1.1

1   Project failure case studies – Lessons learned from other people's mistakes – v1.8 by Henrico Dolfing

2   https://www.pmi.org/learning/library/ navigating-complexity-project-culture-10181

1.2

1   Repa, K. (2013). Planning for program closeout. Paper presented at PMI® Global Congress 2013—North America, New Orleans, LA. Newtown Square, PA: Project Management Institute. (*https://www.pmi.org/learning/ library/planning-program-closeout-5844*)

1.3

1   The Project Book – The complete guide to consistently delivering great projects – Colin D Ellis (Wiley)

2   *https://xebia.com/blog/the-legend-of-the-5-monkeys-the-doctor-and-the-rose/*

3   *https://hbr.org/2015/05/how-to-be-an-effective-executive-sponsor*

4   *https://www.mckinsey.com/business-functions/organization/our-insights/ getting-personal-about-change*

5   *https://passthehoney.com/blogs/the-buzz/how-do-bees-make-hives*

6   *https://journals.sagepub.com/doi/full/10.1177/2158244020914590#*

7   The Five Dysfunctions of a team – Patrick Lencioni

8   The Fearless Organisation – Amy C Edmondson

9   world without bees – *https://www.youtube.com/watch?v=7X1xllyZw3M*

10 *https://www.brightwork.com/blog/ project-failures-londons-1m-per-month-millennium-dome*

11 'How Gap Inc. Engaged with its Stakeholders' (*MIT Sloan Management Review*) *https://sloanreview.mit.edu/article/ how-gap-inc-engaged-with-its-stakeholders/*

12 winning partnership: Financial institutions and strategic suppliers – *https://www.mckinsey.com/industries/financial-services/ our-insights/a-winning-partnership-financial-institutions-and-strategic-suppliers*

13 *https://www.stuff.co.nz/business/industries/63368788/ auckland-councils-70m-it-blowout*

14 Final House Committee report on the Boeing 737 Max – *https://www. washingtonpost.com/context/final-house-committee-report-on-the-boeing-737- max/2ab7a376-79ec-4da4-bf0f-f7a4ecf8f4af/?itid=lk_interstitial_manual_5*

15 Project failure case studies – Lessons learned from other people's mistakes – v1.8 by Henrico Dolfing

1.4

1 *https://www.espncricinfo.com/story/alex-hales-dropped-from-england-s- world-cup-squad-following-drugs-ban-1182533*

2 'The journey to an agile organization at Zalando' published on McKinsey. com – *https://www.mckinsey.com/business-functions/organization/ our-insights/the-journey-to-an-agile-organization-at-zalando*

1.5

1 The article 'Elephant on thin ice: Navigating complexity through project culture' published by the Project Management Institute. Focus on the acknowledgment part more than anything else. *https://www.pmi.org/ learning/library/navigating-complexity-project-culture-10181*

1.6

1 How do bees make hives? – *https://passthehoney.com/blogs/the-buzz/ how-do-bees-make-hives*

2 Finite and infinite games – A vision of life as play and possibility – James P. Carse – Free Press

1.7

3 Executive Sponsor Engagement: Top Driver of Project and Program Success – *https://www.pmi.org/learning/thought-leadership/pulse/ top-driver-project-program-success*

4 The Emperor's New Clothes – *https://en.wikipedia.org/wiki/ The_Emperor%27s_New_Clothes*

5 Project Failures: London's £1M Per-Month Millennium Dome –

6 *https://www.brightwork.com/blog/ project-failures-londons-1m-per-month-millennium-dome*

2.2

1 The project rots from the head – Colin D Ellis – *https://www.colindellis. com/books/the-project-rots-from-the-head*

2 US Airways Flight 1549 – *https://en.wikipedia.org/wiki/US_Airways_ Flight_1549#:~:text=Unable%20to%20reach%20any%20airport,with%20 a%20few%20serious%20injuries.*

3 data-backed approach to stakeholder engagement – *https:// www.mckinsey.com/business-functions/organization/our-insights/ the-organization-blog/a-data-backed-approach-to-stakeholder-engagement*

2.3

1 The making of men – Dr. Arne Rubenstein

2 Make milestones matter with 'decision gates' — stage gates with real teeth – *https://www.mckinsey.com/business-functions/operations/our-insights/ make-milestones-matter-with-decision-gatesstage-gates-with-real-teeth*

2.4

1 Managing project teams in an age of complexity – *https://www.pmi.org/ learning/library/managing-project-teams-age-complexity-7212*

2.5

1 McKinsey article on Digitising the delivery of government services – *https:// www.mckinsey.com/business-functions/mckinsey-digital/our-insights/ digitizing-the-delivery-of-government-services*

2.6

1 Company values – *https://www.atlassian.com/company/values*

2 How to communicate effectively in times of uncertainty – *https:// www.mckinsey.com/business-functions/organization/our-insights/ the-organization-blog/how-to-communicate-effectively-in-times-of-uncertainty*

3 Vodafone EVO programme – *https://www.accenture.com/gr-en/~/ media/Accenture/Conversion-Assets/DotCom/Documents/Global/PDF/ Technology_5/Accenture-EVO-Vodafone-Business-Transformation-Programme.pdf*

2.7

1 PMBOK® Guide and Standards – *https://www.pmi.org/pmbok-guide-standards*

2 The article 'The science of uncertainty: Blown budgets and destroyed schedules? Sometimes, it's weak project estimation that's to blame' published by Project Management Institute – *https://www.pmi.org/learning/library/science-uncertainty-project-estimation-11520*

3.1

1 Thought Leaders – *https://thoughtleaders.com.au/*

2 The Bridge On The River Choluteca – *http://www.businessworld.in/article/The-Bridge-on-the-River-Choluteca/23-08-2020-311912/*

3 Sydney opera house – *https://www.sydneyoperahouse.com/*

4 Avoiding the successful failure – *https://www.pmi.org/learning/library/avoiding-successful-failure-triple-constraints-7344*

5 The five dysfunctions of a team – Patrick C. Lencioni

6 Case study: The Millennium Dome in 'Project failure case studies and suggestion', published in the International Journal of Computer Applications – *https://www.researchgate.net/publication/262952882_Project_Failure_Case_Studies_and_Suggestion*

3.2

1 The human factor in project management' published by Project Management Institute – *https://www.pmi.org/learning/library/human-factor-project-management-9276*

3.3

1 LEVI Strauss's SAP implementation and budget overruns – *https://www.zdnet.com/article/levi-strauss-sap-rollout-substantially-hurt-quarter/*

4.1

1 The war of art – Steven Pressfield

About the author

Ganapathy Iyer is a leading project manager and mentor, based in Auckland, New Zealand. He works with organisations to structure and deliver great projects. He mentors, coaches and trains people to setup and deliver great project results.

He has led and delivered a host of large, complex technology-enabled transformation projects, across geographies, often working with multicultural and diverse teams.

He believes that projects are the lifeline of organisational and individual growth, and is committed to making the world of projects a great place to be.

Some of the projects he has been involved in include Vodafone Group's global ERP SAP rollout across India, Ghana, New Zealand, South Africa, Auckland Council's Human Capital Management project, and the NewCore programme.

He holds a post-graduate management qualification from T.A. Pai Management Institute in India. He is also a qualified Electrical Engineer, a certified Project Management Professional (PMP®) and a Certified ScrumMaster (CSM®).

Ganapathy has lived in New Zealand since 2013 with his wife Dipali and their son Balaark. He loves the energising and balanced lifestyle that New Zealand provides, where you can do great work and enjoy life on equal terms. He is an avid cricket fan and a Bollywood music lover.

He loves sharing his knowledge and experiences gained on projects, working with great people on projects and is committed to helping individuals and organisations infuse joy and fun into projects to enable great outcomes for everyone.